The new service society

The new service society

Russell Lewis

Longman

LONGMAN GROUP LIMITED
London

*Associated companies, branches and representatives
throughout the world*

First published* 1973

ISBN 0 582 46061 1

*Printed in Hong Kong by
Dai Nippon Printing Co (Int.) Ltd*

Contents

To Alys

1

The coming service society: prospects for the year 2000

In the year 2000, barring major folly or catastrophe, the United States should be overwhelmingly a service society. For if present trends continue, almost three-quarters of America's workers will earn their living in services by the century's end. To the layman this statement may be mildly surprising, but not wildly exciting. If he is a layman who cares, he may reasonably ask how Americans employ their working hours now. And what in any case is a service? The answers to these questions, we must hope, will reveal that this development in the world's most advanced economy – and the one which should continue to serve as the trendsetter for the rest – is no mere statistical curiosity, but a momentous transformation with profound economic, social, political, cultural and even psychological and spiritual consequences. Here we are concerned, above all, to show that western politics in general, and British politics in particular, have failed to adjust to this crucial and historic change. On the contrary it has been until recently the perverse aim of most democratic politicians to foster the development of a big, bureaucratic, corporate style of government which was certainly never very alluring and forfeits whatever justification it originally had, now that the relative importance of industry in the economy is on the wane.

Let us take the last question first; what is a service? Definition is harder than it looks. The commonsense notion is that as wealth consists of goods and services, the distinction between them is that goods are material and tangible and services are immaterial and intangible. Yet the great neoclassical economist Alfred Marshall made the following rather disconcerting observation:

Man cannot create material things. In the mental and moral world indeed he may produce new ideas; but when he is said to produce material things, he really only produces utilities or in other words his efforts and sacrifices result in changing the form or arrangement of matter to adapt it better for the satisfaction of wants. All that he can do in the physical world is either to readjust matter so as to make it more useful, as when he makes a log of wood into a table; or to put it on the way of being made more useful by nature, as when he puts seed where the forces of nature will make it burst out into life.[1]

Marshall went on to chide those who said that traders were non-producers, for there was no scientific foundation for any distinction between the activities of the cabinet maker and the furniture dealer, between the railwayman carrying coal above ground and the miner carrying it under ground, or between the fisherman and the fishmonger. All produced utilities and could do no more. As for those who revived the medieval attack on traders as parasites, they merely missed the mark. There might be too many traders but that reflected the imperfect organisation of trade, particularly retail trade. Marshall, as usual, went to the heart of the matter: the distinction between goods and services is not fundamental and certainly not moral (even if production is moral), it is classificatory, and the classification is to be judged by its convenience which means partly by the extent of its acceptance in use. Unhappily, as George J. Stigler has said, 'There exists no authoritative consensus on either the boundaries or the classification of the service industries.'[2] In his authoritative study of the service economy Victor R. Fuchs excludes transportation, communications and public utilities and places them in the industry sector 'because of their dependence upon heavy capital equipment and complex technology'.[3] The remaining services are characterised by being manned by white-collar workers, usually labour-intensive, mostly dealing with the consumer and producing an intangible product. Fuchs further distinguishes a 'service sub-sector' which excludes government, households and institutions, and real estate. Broadly this is the private enterprise part of his service sector and its final output can be more reliably measured than most services. For us this would be too restricting: services have a collectivist as well as a free market significance. In any event there is enough scope for arguing the finer points of such definitions to delight a medieval theologian. For present purposes it is just as well to stick to the official classifications used by those pragmatic pundits, the national income statisticians. A table from the *US Annual Ab-*

[1] Alfred Marshall, *Principles of Economics*, 8th edn, Macmillan, 1947, p. 62.
[2] George J. Stigler, *Trends in Employment in the Service Industries*, Princeton University Press for National Bureau of Economic Research, 1956, p. 47.
[3] Victor R. Fuchs, *The Service Economy*, National Bureau of Economic Research, 1968, p. 16.

stract provides the argument of this book with a suitable statistical point of departure.

		Non-agricultural Employment by sector			
		1965 million		2000 million	
GOODS	(Mining	0.6)		0.5)	
	(	)		)	
	(Manufacturing	18.0)	36%	24.2)	25%
	(	)		)	
	(Construction (Contract)	3.2)		6.5)	
SERVICES	(Transportation and utilities	4.0)		5.9)	
	(	)		)	
	(Wholesale and retail trade	12.6)		35.0)	
	(	0)		)	
	(Finance and real estate	3.0)	64%	5.9)	75%
	(	)		)	
	(Miscellaneous services	8.9)		34.0)	
	(	)		)	
	(Government	10.1)		14.6)	
	TOTAL	60.4	100%	126.6	100%

Source: *US Statistical Abstract*, 1966, p. 221.

This forecast must be of interest to all other countries because, to judge by past experience America, economically at least, is their tomorrow and America's tomorrow is only their day after that. Nor do their expectations rest on the American example alone, for the faster growth of service employment was clearly in evidence in most advanced countries well before the Second World War, and the trend has continued ever since. Thus, for example, in the European Community's first decade service employment there rose from 34.5 to 40.2 per cent of the total.

Nor is this all. Very roughly the proportion of services in the economy corresponds with the degree of affluence. Certainly, at the extremes, the relationship holds very well. Thus, the USA is at the top of the ladder, with 59 per cent of her workers in services, while on the bottom rungs are Spain, 32 per cent, Portugal 32 per cent, Greece 28 per cent and Turkey 16 per cent. Italy, the poorest country in the Common Market, also has the lowest ratio of service workers. The Soviet Union's proportion of service workers is about the same as Spain's. Admittedly the link with the standard of living is inexact in the middle range. For instance, West Germany, with 41 per cent, actually has a higher standard of living than the United Kingdom, with 49 per cent, and a considerably higher standard than Japan with 46 per cent.[1]

Yet, on reflection, it would be rather surprising if the prominence of a country's service sector were to tally precisely with its affluence rating. For though some service activities, such as computer programming, obviously belong to a modern economy, the heyday of others, for example domestic service, coincided with the earlier episodes of *The Forsyte Saga*. Thus, while it is said that three-quarters of the scientists who have ever lived are still alive, the number of household servants in Great Britain has been declining more or less since the beginning of the First World War. Indeed service employment while expanding steadily overall presents in detail a most varied picture ranged from bounding vigour to doddering decline. The more dynamic service groups in rough order of dynamism are, first, business services, such as banking, insurance, advertising, and estate management; secondly, professional and scientific services, a kind of mélange of the traditional and the hypermodern; thirdly, a miscellany of amenity services such as sport, recreation, gambling, hairdressing and motor servicing; and fourthly, the Civil Services both local and national. At the other end of the scale the prime examples of decadence are old-fashioned personal services, especially domestic (butlers grow more precious year by year), laundering and cobbling, and, that prime casualty of the television era, the cinema.

Such then, in brief, is the shape of the developing service economy. The mundane homely character of many of these changes should not be permitted to shroud the reality that here is one of the great movements of economic history, though one strangely neglected by many who should be professionally concerned. Its neglect is all the more surprising since it is so much the custom of history textbook writers to treat our economic past as a continuous flow only broken by certain watersheds representing the newly dominant mode of production. Thus, according to the conventional scheme, through most of recorded history the main sources of wealth were the primary activities of farming, fishing and mining. The agricultural revolution which began in England was the precondition of an even greater revolution in industry which by the end of the nineteenth century had overtaken all the nations of what we now call the western world. America first reached the high watermark of industrialism in the

[1] *Basic Statistics of the Community*, 1971.

roaring 'twenties, for America invented not merely the so-called durables or mass consumer goods but the mass consumer as well. It was
not until the late 1950s in Western Europe, and the mid 1960s in
Japan, that the mass consumption society came into its own. The
Soviet bloc's ruling elite even now hesitate to commit themselves to
such a change, which would inevitably confer greater freedom on the
masses and might weaken their own power. Moreover, compared
with the earlier stage of industrialisation, the mass consumption
phase is far more difficult to plan. The Soviet system's defeat over
the durables may come to rival its failure on the farms. Meanwhile,
as the industrialisation of the whole world proceeds, North America,
followed at a distance by other Western nations and Japan, is moving
into an entirely different style of society, in which, in employment
terms if not in terms of output, industry will in the next century be no
more important than agriculture is now. For the automatic factory
is already with us, even if it is not in widespread use, and continuing
advances in electronics, especially in computers, must have radical
labour-saving effects. Already the process is well advanced. To
quote Michael Harrington: 'In 1964 ten men could produce as many
automobile blocks as 400 men in 1954; two workers could make
1,000 radios a day, a job that required 200 a few years before; 14
operators were tending the glassblowing machines that manufactured 90 per cent of all the glass bulbs in the USA.

Daniel Bell has christened what America threatens to be in the
year 2000 'the post-industrial society' and makes the main defining
characteristic the advancement to a level of *per capita* income of
£4000 per year. The term 'service society' is, we contend, more useful
because it refers to the economic activity in which most people will
be employed.

Whether services will represent an ever more substantial proportion of total output is less certain. According to Fuchs the service
sector's share of total employment in America has been steadily
rising (from 40 per cent in 1929 to over 55 per cent in 1967) its share
of output has not – even measured in current dollars it grew only
from 47 to 50 per cent.[1] It is true that Fuchs's definition of services is
narrower than that used by national income statisticians because it
excludes public utilities and transport. But even on the wider definition the conclusion would not be greatly different. Fuchs believes
the relatively slow growth in the productivity of services is due
to not one but several factors. There was a greater fall in hours
worked per man in services than industry. Then there was a relative

[1] Michael Harrington, *The Accidental Century* (Pelican), 1967, p. 194.

rise in the quality of the industrial labour force – in effect an increase in human capital. Finally there was a much larger increase in physical capital per worker in industry. He also suggests that technological change in industry was more rapid than in services and that the gain from growing economies of scale was greater.[1]

Yet there is good reason for thinking that the productivity growth of services will not continue to lag but, in many cases, accelerate dramatically. Technological advances of recent years are opening up, on a wide front, opportunities for profitable investment in labour-saving equipment and techniques. In transport the growth of pipelines should displace a great deal of comparatively labour-intensive road haulage. Again with containerisation and palletisation merchant ships on the Atlantic run, which actually used to spend 70 per cent of their lives in port, may reduce this to as little as 20 per cent, as they can now be turned round in a matter of hours instead of days. At Tilbury, for instance, the *American Lancer,* the United States' Lines first container ship built for the purpose, was turned round in eleven hours. In that time thirteen men discharged and loaded some 4000 tons, a task which would have required 120 men operating on a conventional piecemeal cargo basis.[2]

Electronic control is already doing a great deal to improve the efficiency of railways. In New York the City Transit Authority has been running a driverless train since 1962. On many railway systems automatic control and marshalling of goods wagons is well advanced.

There is bound to be major capital investment in telecommunications 'in the next twenty years. Most technically advanced countries will build national electronic networks for communications, just as they have built networks for the supply of electric power.'[3] The telephone network will, in time, be linked in with the grid, which will also carry radio and television programmes plus information exchange on a tremendous scale, and will eventually be used for the electronic transmission of letters, newspapers and books. This will mean a colossal saving of human time. It should also economise on personal transport, because, if communications are so good, many people will be able to work at home.

In distribution the supermarket is already showing the way to cut labour costs drastically where the scale of operation is sufficiently

[1] Victor R. Fuchs, *The Service Economy,* p. 5.
[2] G. Van Den Burg, *Containerisation, a modern transport system,* Hutchinson, 1969, p. 147.
[3] S. Handel, *The Electronic Revolution,* Penguin (Pelican), 1967, p. 126.

large. Automated grocery or department stores, which are just as feasible in principle as the automatic factory, would certainly need less shop assistants.

The Giro system, again, is only the beginning of a changeover which must in time lead to a chequeless, paperless, computerised form of banking. This will be necessary if only because the volume of paper is becoming indigestible – already the British clearing banks handle over 1000 million cheques a year. Electronic banking will reduce the need for clerks just as a cashless system, which is a longer-term possibility, should do away with the need for cashiers. The same sort of staff saving should be achievable by the use of electronic accounting in insurance companies, while the cumbersome system of share transfer on the stock exchange cries out for reform.

Professional services might seem to be the most resistant of all to any attempts to raise their productivity. How does one raise the productivity of a judge? In fact there is more scope than meets the eye. If all legal cases were filed in a computer, and made quickly retrievable and analysable, judges might well make more rapid, better-quality judgments. There might even be–shades of Capek–an electronic judge.

In education, ignoring the awesome prospect of implanting knowledge surgically, there must be considerable scope for replacing teachers with teaching machines, at least where the sheer drudgery of learning is concerned.

Medical services may become less labour-intensive, too. Apparently, by the use of an 'electronic nurse', which involves attaching to each patient lightweight transducers on the appropriate parts of the body, it will be possible for one human nurse to supervise hundreds of patients from a central control panel.[1] Diagnosis of illnesses by a central computer should also increase the productivity of doctors.

Among miscellaneous services the most striking example is an activity where the prospect for the substitution of capital equipment for labour looks most bleak, namely domestic service. Ignoring the more obvious labour-saving household gadgets which after all still have not done away with many people's need for a 'daily', according to Professor M.W. Thring,[2] it should be quite possible at a development cost of £1 million to produce a robot slave in ten years. This creature could be programmed to carry out a number of routine household chores like scrubbing, sweeping, dusting, washing-up,

[1] S. Handel, *The Electronic Revolution*, p. 204.
[2] Nigel Calder, ed., *The World in 1984*, vol. 2, Penguin (Pelican), 1965, p. 39.

laying tables and making beds.

It is plainly not feasible to quantify the effect of all these possible changes in the efficiency of workers in services, the reactions on prices, expenditures, and employment, and, hence, the relative place of services in western economies over the next generation. It seems likely, however, that services will become more abundant and cheaper and that people will buy more of them. In that case economic historians of the future will find their subject matter slotting into a sequence which is a veritable pedagogue's delight. Man's economic evolution will appear as a series of qualitative changes in the dominant form of final output. The sequence might be like this: phase one, agricultural; phase two, the industrial revolution; phase three, mass consumption; phase four, the service society. The economist, as well as the historian of the future, should by then be better disposed towards services because he should be using an economic theory as well as statistical material, which is capable of measuring service activity objectively, and which is not biased, as our contemporary economic theory and statistical treatments regrettably are, in favour of goods.

The most important change of outlook needed is in the legitimisation of services as valid forms of wealth, the recognition that they are the sources of affluence, not the candy floss diet of an affluent society. The appreciation of this truth will have consequences of the widest importance for both economic analysis and policy. It was a broadly correct rule in the past that the way for a country to become rich was to industrialise. So in the future the way for an already industrialised country to become still richer will be to learn the techniques and conform to the *mores* of a service society. It might appear that such a statement only needs making in order to command universal assent. Unhappily this is not so. On the contrary there are many politicians and, worse still, economists and intellectuals, who refuse to be enlightened. Perhaps like Scott Fitzgerald's Gatsby they only believe in the green light, in the orgastic future that year by year recedes before them and, like him, are borne back ceaselessly into the past. It is to such nostalgic confusions that we must now turn.

Note: The statistical background for the discussion in this chapter is provided in the Appendix on p. 164.

2

Old myths die hard:
the need for reappraisal

A powerful and insidious myth pervades and perverts the economic policies of many otherwise sophisticated modern states, the myth that intangible services which are fleeting are morally inferior to physical goods which endure. Among western countries since the Second World War it has found what must be its strongest expression in both the theory and the practice of the British Labour Party. Thus that austere economic puritan Sir Stafford Cripps stated (29 February 1946): 'Prewar we had nearly three million people in distribution producing nothing.' It is not surprising that Labour's four year economic plan (for the years 1948–52) did not mention distribution among the headings of sectors to which capital investment was to be steered. And the practice lived up to the theory. The chief instrument of control, the building licence, was used so as to hamper severely investment in shops[1] and for that matter in offices (except government ones) and cinemas, all of which, like that favourite haunt of Bertie Wooster's, the Drones' Club, fell into the same luckless category of 'non-producers'.[2]

Admittedly such discrimination was not new, it carried forward into times of peace the priorities of war, according to which the building of shops, offices and cinemas was classified among the inessentials. Such continuity sprang from the fact that the machinery of war-time planning was left intact.

The sheer inertia of the planners and officials, ruled by criteria, not of consumer satisfaction, but of victory, might therefore account for the inherited antiservice priorities which governed the issue of licences to build. Thus the effect of ideological prejudice in high places was, perhaps mainly, to buttress bureaucratic inertia. The antiservice myth reinforced the conservatism of official routine, and

[1] J.C.R. Dow, *The Management of the British Economy 1945–60*, NIESR CUP, 1965, p. 152.
[2] Bertie Wooster was not only a non-producer. He was also an employer of a most efficient service sector named 'Jeeves'.

delayed a rational reappraisal of a pattern of behaviour imposed by the necessities of war.[1]

The subsequent Labour administration of Mr Harold Wilson could be regarded as a more genuine test case of the influence of the myth. The wartime apparatus of controls had been largely scrapped during the 1950s. If the bias of Labour once more in power was to be exercised against services the area of policy where that bias would most easily apply was taxation. That is why the appointment of Professor Nicholas Kaldor (who was among other things an expert on the theory of taxation) as special economic adviser to Mr Wilson's Government was so significant. He was the principal advocate of fiscal discrimination against services, which he saw as a means of promoting economic growth. In a nutshell his theory was that fast economic growth was almost invariably associated with a rapidly growing manufacturing sector, which in turn coincided with swiftly expanding employment in manufacturing. Not surprisingly he thought the first essential for British economic policy was the movement of workers out of slow growing low productivity services into fast growing, high productivity manufactures. Yet a major weakness in Professor Kaldor's argument was that it failed to demonstrate the causal link through which a growing labour force creates growth. Indeed it is hard to square the Kaldor theory with present experience in which the squeeze on profits has produced an exceptionally fast rise in industrial productivity at a time when the labour force is static, output is stagnant and employment in industry is falling sharply. The point is simple. It is at least as likely that a fast growth of productivity in manufacturing enables prices to be kept low, wages high, demand and output to rise rapidly then pulling in labour. The idea that the same results can be achieved by pushing in labour is, on the face of it, rather odd. Indeed an excess supply of labour available for use in industry does not, at first sight, seem likely to encourage extra capital investment, on which productivity to some extent depends. If labour is plentiful and cheap the incentive to use it efficiently is surely reduced. On the other hand, if for other reasons labour can be used efficiently and profitably then a ready supply may be advantageous.

Labour availability is a necessary condition for the rapid expansion of industry, hence its statistical presence where industry has expanded rapidly (its absence where industry has not expanded rapidly is hard to establish). But it is not a sufficient condition on its own.

[1] Non-economists may prefer to skip the following brief history and analysis of recent British tax discrimination against services and resume on page 17.

The parallel with the balance of payments is striking. Deflation will release resources to improve the balance of payments and a supply of resources is a necessary condition for any improvement. But it requires something more to cause those resources to shift, otherwise they will simply stand idle. Or to approach the matter in a different way, growth might result from better marketing of manufactures, and if industry is overmanned the formula for progress and expanding production may be the shedding of labour, the reduction of unit costs and the stimulation of sales through lower prices and higher profits. In such a case the original impetus towards growth would come from a growth in the sales force, that is from expansion of employment in services. As a matter of fact this model seems to be very near the mark for the British economy in the 1950s and '60s.

The late William W. Allen, an American consultant, caused something of a sensation in 1964 by asserting that Britain was only working halftime and that the most striking inefficiency was in the industry sector. By international standards the efficiency of British retailing is more impressive than that of British manufacturing: Marks and Spencer is better organised than British Leyland. Besides, as shown in the last chapter, the general trend among modern economies is for the proportion of total employment in services to grow. It is hard to believe that so universal and so well established a tendency can be merely perverse.

More fundamentally the distinction between goods and services, while useful for descriptive purposes, is unrealistic from an operational or policy point of view. It makes no economic sense to rate the contribution of computer hardware as more valuable than that of the software without which it is useless. To do so is, as Professor Jewkes has observed, like distinguishing between the contribution to the progress of a motor car of its back and front wheels. Unfortunately Professor Kaldor's pronouncements provided academically respectable attire for those who had prejudices about the moral worth and 'unproductive' role of services in the economy. It was a still greater misfortune that circumstances conspired to provide the opportunity for these theoretical notions to be embodied in two of Labour's most important tax innovations, namely the substitution of investment grants for allowances, and still more portentously, the selective employment tax.

The main purpose of the cash grants for investment introduced in 1966 was to create a more effective stimulus than the previous tax allowances. It was also the intention to steer that investment into manufacturing in the belief that this would make the most useful contribution towards improving the balance of payments, and increasing the rate of economic growth. In an intriguing paragraph the white paper criticised the old allowances for allowing investment to be too widely dispersed 'in items which have little or no relation to productive investment', and instanced purchases of curtains and carpets in offices, cutlery in works and office canteens and television sets rented out to the public because the purchase of the set by the rental firm qualified. By contrast the cash grants were to be concentrated on plant and machinery in manufacturing extractive and constructional industries.

It may be that one should not take the wording of the white paper too seriously. The terms of the argument may even have been merely a sop to Professor Kaldor, though in reality only providing a ready rationalisation of a procedure which mainly recommended itself on grounds of administrative convenience. Discrimination in favour of industrial plant only can be found as early as 1937 in the mills and factories depreciation allowance, which was confined to mill and factory buildings. The same applied to Mr Maudling's 1963 scheme for free depreciation in development districts. The important novelty of the cash allowances was thus not the crude bias in favour of industry but the introduction of a centrally administered as opposed to a devolved system, that is one which depends in detail on discretionary decisions by officials instead of resting mainly on the interpretation of the rules affecting them by the business men concerned. Because of the range and complexity of the economy the cash grants, if spread over everything, had to be either very expensive or negligible in size. Alternatively by being concentrated not only could they be larger but, it was easier for those administering them to apply the rules. In any event the discrimination was more certainly anomalous and economically distorting than the allowances had been. Computer software which had qualified for the allowances failed to make the grade for grants.

Yet the problem was not administratively insuperable. It would have been feasible to retain the allowances while using the grants in addition to encourage investment by any laggard firm which tickled the bureaucrats' fancy. It is the fact that such a course was not resorted to which demonstrates the strength of the myth of the subordinacy of services. To politicians who believed passionately in purposive intervention a principle of discrimination so ubiquitous and with such appealing moral overtones was not to be lightly discarded.

The selective employment tax (SET) as its name implied was more blatantly explicit in its aim of discriminating against services. According to the white paper, SET sought, by taxing employment in services, to achieve these objectives:

1. To correct the unbalance of existing taxation which fell heavily on manufacturers (e.g. purchase tax) and only lightly on services.
2. To improve the balance of payments by taxing services and keeping a large part of the proceeds, at least in the first instance, as a premium to manufacturing which generated most of Britain's exports.
3. To promote growth and productivity by its relatively favourable treatment of manufacturing, because it was 'upon this sector that the growth of the economy and its ability to meet competition primarily depend' (Cmd 2986).

On further scrutiny, however, these official grounds are not very convincing. First, if the object was fiscal neutrality, i.e. fairness between economic sectors, why not adopt the value added tax which is nearer to neutrality, not only between activities but also between factor inputs? Even if this was not possible, because time was pressing and the government could not wait, there was still the further alternative of a non-discriminatory employment tax.

Second, it did not necessarily follow that the balance of payments would benefit from SET even if manufacturing, the chief source of exports, stood to gain. First because price increases, albeit in service industries, initially tended to be transmitted to the general level of prices. Secondly because the import content of service exports was only 9 per cent against 18 per cent for manufacturing. The net contribution of service exports to the balance of payments in relation to unit value was greater. Also the export volume was surprisingly high amounting to roughly two-fifths of the nation's total exports. The more compelling export thesis was that the subsidy to manufactures from the SET proceeds was a clever way around the GATT prohibition of direct subventions to exporters. At best, this policy only amounted to a concealed devaluation. An open devaluation, as events were to prove, was much more effective.

Third, SET was supposed to contribute to growth according to the afore-mentioned Kaldorian thesis. Yet it is hard to believe that this was much more than a courtesy bow in Professor Kaldor's direction. For the government economists were fully aware of the studies of comparative productivity between services and manufactures by C.H. Feinstein and Lady Margaret Hall or G.D.N. Worswick and C.G. Kane and D.C. Comer[1] all of which were

---

[1] Summarised in *The Case Against the Selective Employment Tax* by the Industrial Policy Group, 1970.

decidedly flattering to services. It was a tribute to the power of the anti-service myth that the evidence could be so blithely ignored, or, rather, it indicated the ability of myth to buttress an irrational policy when that policy suits the books of enough political and departmental interests. For the real as opposed to the alleged reason for the adoption of SET was, for a start, that it was useful to Mr Wilson as a way of fudging the fact that he was breaking a promise he made at the general election only two months earlier that there would be no severe increase in taxation. Equally important it appealed on two different grounds which broadly reflected the two schools of thought which corresponded but only very roughly to the two economic ministries, through which Labour attempted to govern the British economy. It found favour with the Treasury which wanted to raise taxes and reduce demand. It received the blessing of the Department of Economic Affairs which sought to encourage exports, growth and productivity.

As the adoption of SET was the result of political expediency its application was the result of administrative convenience. The administrators faced two problems, first that of classification of activities to which the tax should or should not apply. This was settled by statistical convention, more or less according to the standard industrial classification. The second problem was to determine which establishments fitted which classification. This was settled by the rather crude criterion of whether manufacturing or service workers were in the majority in the establishment concerned. This yielded a rich crop of anomalies.

Taxing services was supposed to boost economic efficiency. Yet the criteria for both SET and the investment grants discriminated in favour of manufacturing and against repairs,[1] thus creating a bias towards waste.

Again, because whole establishments classified as either 'manufacturing' or 'services' according to which activity claimed a majority of the workers, firms which hived off service departments to outside concerns were penalised, though such devolution is often conducive to greater efficiency. Further, the categories to which SET applied were necessarily arbitrary and not always uninfluenced by considerations of political expediency. Thus newspapers and journals (presumably out of a desire not to offend powerful critics) were labelled 'manufacturing' when they did their own printing. Some bodies classified as charities and were exempt; others, not always

[1] J.B. Bracewell, Milnes's article 'Fiscal discrimination between industries,' *Journal of Economic Studies*, July 1968.

for the clearest of reasons, were not. Thus one of the celebrated achievements of SET in its early days was to tax the Salvation Army while paying a premium to the publishers of *Playboy Magazine*.

In another case there were two cafés next door to each other. One charged 1*s* 9*d* for egg and chips, the other 2*s* 3*d*. The first had a bakery attached and therefore received the premium. The second was only a café and therefore paid the tax.

Professor Reddaway began his assessment of the effect of SET in the distributive trades[1] by repudiating the assumption on which the tax was originally based, namely that service industries are inferior to manufacturing. However, he offered a different justification that SET may have raised productivity in the firms to which it applied. Unfortunately, as *The Economist* was quick to point out, there was no necessary causal connection between the rise in productivity in distribution and the imposition of SET which coincided with it. For, apart from the labour shortage, which could alone have produced this effect, SET came into operation during the years when Edward Heath's repeal of resale price maintenance was probably having its maximum impact. Indeed Professor Reddaway admitted that it was not really possible to separate these effects.

Even assuming that SET did increase the productivity of the distributive traders, that would scarcely justify the selective principle. For, as was mentioned earlier, massive labour wastage occurs in manufacturing. (In fact when manufacturing profits were squeezed by a wage explosion from 1969-70 there was a dramatic rise in productivity.) As to the cause, there is no mystery. The fault lies with restrictive labour practices. So, if we accept Professor Reddaway's optimistic conclusion that SET has actually raised productivity in services, surely it should be allowed to confer the same boon on industry, where the wastage of manpower is chronic. Indeed the premium paid to manufacturing under the original SET arrangement was the reverse of what was really required.

The British Labour Government was latterly spending roughly £250 million a year on regional development policies. It was no small matter, therefore, that these policies too were grounded in massive prejudice against service development, though in fact most new jobs occur in the service trades. Even before Labour's arrival in office in 1964 the official assumption was that the essence of a policy for the regions was to tempt or even compel manufacturing industry to migrate to them. The prime instrument of coercion was

[1] W.B. Reddaway, *Effects of SET: Distributive Trades*, HMSO, March 1970.

the industrial development certificate, which was often withheld for projects in Birmingham, London and the South East in order to force captains of industry into opening factories in the North East, the North West or the Celtic fringe. In the early 1960s there was some resentment of the way that office employment escaped from this constraint. A White Paper in 1963 showed that of roughly 40,000 jobs created each year in the London conurbation, only 20 per cent were in manufacturing industry.

Labour seized on this gladly and passed an act controlling office development in 1965. Yet though anxiety over congestion may have inspired this move this was reinforced by dislike of London offices, which radical propaganda had frequently represented as examples of frivolous misdirection of resources under affluent capitalism when many people were still homeless. Certainly none of Labour's other regional measures suggested much grasp of the key role of services in regional development. Its policy for internal airways, for instance, was more concerned with strengthening the position of British Rail, than with consolidating the dominance of the nationalised air corporations. It disregarded the famous Toothill Report's plea for better air services and more competition on the London and Glasgow/Edinburgh air routes as a vital step in attracting business to Scotland, vital because only easy access to the metropolis would reconcile tycoons to producing on the periphery.

The most favoured instrument of regional bribery under Mr Wilson's regime was the investment grant. Superseding the old investment allowances, these cash grants were paid at the rate of 40 per cent in Development Areas compared with 20 per cent elsewhere, but only for plant or machinery for manufacturing or mining. It was much the same story with the grants and loans available under the Local Employment Acts.

There was a final twist in the continuing story of SET. When the Act first came into force, all manufacturers were repaid their tax plus a 7s 6d premium on each adult male employee. After devaluation this premium was abolished except in development areas, though it disappeared there too as from April 1970. It was followed by a regional employment premium (REP) which enabled Development Area employers in manufacturing industry to claim for a further 30s, making a total of 37s 6d.[1] The result was that the degree of tax discrimination against services became far more marked in the Development Areas than in other parts of the country. Yet, as

---

[1] There is some evidence that REP served less to reduce costs in regions than to boost wages, almost the opposite of what is required for industrial and labour movement.

the CBI pointed out, manufacturing itself cannot grow without corresponding growth in the service industries. An increase in car output, for example, must usually lead to a demand for more petrol stations. Moreover, in Scotland, Wales, Cornwall and other areas tourism is a key sector and one with exciting growth possibilities.

Meanwhile the main limit on the growth of the less prosperous areas has been the lack of such servies as labour training facilities and generally what in the jargon is called, 'poor infrastructure'. Yet what is infrastructure if not a collection of services such as transport, communications, ports, airports and research establishments? With the benefit of hindsight it is now clear that it would have been better for Scottish development to divert the subsidy going to the steel mill at Ravenscraig into a new opera house in Edinburgh or even into cleaning the stone façades on the buildings in central Glasgow. Such improvements in the infrastructure of amenity might do much to raise Scottish morale and make more people feel that Scotland is a good place for visitors to go to or for the natives not to abandon.

We have dwelt on the policies of Britain's Labour Government because they were an extreme reflection of the belief in many powerful quarters that services are, economically speaking, the sweet smell of success rather than success itself. No doubt the error is so widespread among politicians because it has been compounded by intellectuals. It is instructive how even so distinguished a scholar as Professor W. W. Rostow appears to fall into this trap. In his celebrated work, *The Stages of Economic Growth* (1960), having worked his way through to the stage of high mass consumption, when the ownership of automobiles and consumer durables becomes universal, he arrives at a subheading 'Beyond high mass consumption'. Under this he poses the question of what will happen to societies when they have sufficient income to provide more than enough food, decent housing and clothing, and everyone has his own personal transport. After some unilluminating rhetorical questions about possible alternatives he finally asks: 'Or will Man, converted en masse into a suburban version of an eighteenth-century country gentleman, find in some mixture of the equivalent of hunting, shooting and fishing, the life of the mind and spirit, and the minimum drama of carrying forward the human race, sufficient frontiers to keep for life its savour?'

This is the nearest Rostow approaches to an account of the next stage of development, and the details are decidedly meagre. The only inkling he offers of the stupendous prospect for services is thrown off in the phrase 'some mixture of the equivalent of hunting, shooting and fishing'. It is not even clear that services have any part to play in 'the life of the mind and spirit'. Indeed it appears that for Professor Rostow the age of high mass consumption is history's final goal, when mankind, from under a deluge of Cadillacs, dish-washers and electric toothbrushes, proclaims the triumph of the kingdom of freedom over the kingdom of necessity. No wonder, on Rostow's economic interpretation of history, that the way ahead looks so barren, with nothing to look forward to but the battle with boredom and spiritual stagnation.

Still more important in the propagation of myths which obscure the growing importance of the service sector is the work of John Kenneth Galbraith. He is the most talented of the many economists who exaggerate the importance of the manufacturing sector, which in fact only accounts for a quarter of the US national income. His extended work *The New Industrial State* (Hamish Hamilton, 1967) attempts a comprehensive interpretation of the whole trend of American economy and society. As the title implies, the new social order is dominated by industry, and industry is typically governed by the large corporation. This new behemoth manipulates consumer choice through advertising, fixes prices as it chooses, finances large-scale and lucrative research and development, never makes losses, and is run by a managerial élite which cares more for power than profits. It is then but a step to argue that the bases of competitive capitalism have crumbled and that pluralist political democracy, founded on the dispersion of economic power, has decayed.

It follows that the only way for democracy to survive in the company of the corporate giants is to create a countervailing corporate state, which vests huge discretionary powers in the governing élite of politicians and bureaucrats, to enable them to engage in large-scale planning and control. The fact that Galbraith exaggerates the monopoly power of the big concerns even in the industrial sector of the economy only makes the myth appear more devastating. Unfortunately too the notion that business is the domain of a small band of manufacturing monopolies flatters popular prejudice. As Milton Friedman points out[1] there is a tendency to confuse absolute and relative size. So, as big enterprises grow, they are assumed to occupy more of the market, though the market may in fact be growing still faster. Further he says 'monopoly is newsworthy and leads to more attention than competition'. The illustration he gives is most apt in the present context. He goes on:

[1] *Capitalism and Freedom*, the University of Chicago Press (Phoenix books), p. 122.

If individuals were asked to list the major industries in the United States, almost all would include automobile production, few would include wholesale trade. Yet wholesale trade is twice as important as automobile production. Wholesale trade is highly competitive hence draws little attention to itself. Automobile production, while in certain respects highly competitive, has many fewer firms and is certainly closer to monopoly. Everyone can name the leading firms producing automobiles.

The impression that even manufacturing industry consists of a few enormous firms, steadily growing in scale, is indeed largely false. In 1963 there were roughly a quarter of a million separate manufacturing firms in the United States. Over nine-tenths of them employed less than a thousand workers, and these accounted for about a third of all the workers in manufacturing industry. Moreover, there has been little change in the size distribution of industrial firms over the last half-century.[1] It is not even true that the corporation as a form of economic organisation is an increasingly dominant one. On the contrary it appears that the proportion of the U.S. national income which they account for and which was growing until 1956 (when it was 57%) has since been steady or diminishing. This is because of the growing service sector, which is the principal part of the economy, and consists in the main of small firms, including partnerships or other non-corporate types of organisation invariably managed by their owners. Even when it comes to the civil service those employed in local government out-number those in federal and State Government combined.

The comment of Victor R. Fuchs in his pioneering study *The Service Economy*, which is chiefly based on American experience, sums up the position well:

> As these and other facts become known, we may see an end to the myth of the dominance of the large corporation in our society. Most people do not work and never have worked for large corporations; most production does not take place and never has taken place in large corporations. In the future the large corporation is likely to be overshadowed by the hospitals, universities, research institutes, government agencies and professional organisations that are the hall marks of the Service Economy.[2]

Statistics for the decade 1956-66 show some increase in concentration in Britain, but not in Germany or Japan. However, according

[1] Professor J. Jewkes 'The giant corporation in perspective', in *Economic Age*, Jan/Feb 1969, Economic Research Council.
[2] Victor R. Fuchs, *The Service Economy*, p. 10.

to a study by Hart and Prais (*Journal of the Royal Statistical Society*, part 2, 1956) the size distribution of British public companies did not appreciably change in the first half of this century.

The oft-repeated assertion that the large concerns have special advantages of scale in research and development is not borne out by the facts. Thus in the United States between 1959 and 1965 the twenty companies spending most on research and development increased their share of the total net sales of manufactured goods only negligibly, from 18 to 19 per cent.[1] The Industrial Policy Group, a sort of club of the twenty-five or so top businessmen in Britain, say that in their experience competition has never been as intense or as extensive as it is nowadays.[2] The important factors in their view are: the widening range of goods and services available to the consumer; competition between different materials and different processes; competition between firms of different types and sizes and the increasing strength of international competition. They also insist that advertising contributes much more towards stimulating competitive innovation than to protection and monopoly.

Why then, if it is contrary to the evidence, does the myth of the predominance of the giant corporations persist? Partly it is a case of the sheer inertia of the ideas which have become established in the teaching curriculum. Various books like A.A. Berle and G.C. Means's study of *The Modern Corporation* published in the 1930s have become authorities and are hard to shift.

Like the Whig interpretation of history the general doctrine has remainded standing long after the factual foundations have been completely undermined. It is also the fault, on the one hand, of economists, for allowing unrealistic expository devices like the theory of imperfect competition to become substitutes for empirical investigations of industry, and, on the other, of businessmen, for failing to communicate to the academic world the real nature of the situation with which they have had to deal.

Substantially the same case as Galbraith's has been put with diffuse eloquence by the British economist Andrew Shonfield especially in his portentous *Modern Capitalism* (1965). He may be taken as representative of the whole intellectual movement towards 'indicative' or 'soft' planning which originated in France, and has spread even more successfully than other French fashions among the countries of the West. Here again there is a pervading obsession with the

[1] Industrial Policy Group, *The Structure and Efficiency of British Industry*, Research Publications Services, July 1970, p. 12.
[2] Industrial Policy Group, *The Growth of Competition*, Dec. 1970.

behaviour of big industrial firms which, because of their size and the need to take long-term views, plan their own development. As it happens, these industrial mammoths have been confronted every-where in the postwar world with a state greatly enlarged by its res-ponsibilities for welfare and full employment. In assuming a further responsibility for growth, Shonfield believes government is irreluct-ably drawn into a dialogue with big business, with a view to creating a plan for growth and balanced development, behind which the whole of the energies of the nation can be mobilised. The result is the economics of Jean Jacques Rousseau. The profit motive yields to the dynamics of the general will.

Unfortunately the whole scheme of ideas suffers from the impreci-sion of Rousseau's original mystic conception. In practice, indica-tive planning, if we are to judge by the French example, far from being an exercise of the popular will is an autocratic style of govern-ment run by a caucus of bureaucrats and top industrialists – as French trade unionists, for example, have for long and frequently complained.

Why should so many economists of repute either to all intents and purposes ignore services, or assume an actively hostile attitude to them? Part of the answer is that intellectuals are often very conserva-tive about their own specialities. Like generals, they are fully pre-pared to win the last war. Every scholar has a vested interest in the learning he has laboriously acquired. Naturally he is reluctant to see his intellectual capital depreciate. Thus he is psychologically pre-disposed to go on asserting views and dogmas which have long ceased to be valid. Unhappily economists are not exempt from this tendency. It is notorious that the bulk of the profession, when faced with mass unemployment between the wars, cried out that above all the budget must be balanced. We now know that this was the very reverse of what was required. Again, during much of the post-war period British government advisors nurtured on Keynesian economics, consistently recommended policies essentially designed to cure unemployment. Yet the most pressing problem has in fact been inflation and related balance of payment difficulties. So, once more, the cures prescribed have aggravated the disease.

Yet the last generation has not been alone in its perversity. The history of economic thought shows that, as regards the fundamen-tals of their science, economists have almost wilfully refused to move with the times. They have been especially reluctant to admit the existence of new forms of wealth, and when they have accepted it *de facto* they have usually been unwilling to recognise it *de jure*. Like old aristocrats confronted by the nouveaux riches, they spurn what they cannot ignore. And this applies to some of the most eminent as much as to some of the most humble practitioners of the art.

Thus, to go back to the beginnings, Aristotle might be said to have started the whole controversy with his distinction between two forms of value – that arising from nature which was true and that arising from exchange, which was false. Since Aristotle spent twenty years at Plato's Athenian academy; acute observer that he was, he could hardly have failed to perceive that the wealth of the Athenians derived largely from commerce, yet he shrank from giving his approval to this lower form of the art of acquisition. He went on insisting that real wealth was production for the needs of the household, for this was 'natural', exchange was barren and only legitimate when in the primitive form of barter. Retail trade went beyond supplying needs and was unnatural and evil.

Medieval thinking about economics followed closely the lines which Aristotle had laid down, but was modified by the Christian view that the things of this world are of secondary importance since this life is no more than a preparation for the next. Indeed the riches of the world were regarded with suspicion because they might prove a snare, diverting people from the main pursuit which was salvation. The rich man, after all, could take small comfort from the biblical text which compared his chances of passing through the pearly gates with those of a camel penetrating the eye of a needle. It was because the opportunities of the merchant to make money were greater than those of other people – through charging more than the just price for instance, or, even worse, charging usurious interest on a loan – that trade came to be regarded as more corrupt and so less honourable than other occupations. This was natural enough in an economically backward society. Yet, paradoxically, it seems that the attitude of the Church became more rigid as time went on. Usury was at first forbidden to clerics alone. It was only with the commercial revival of the thirteenth century that the prohibition became general and an offence in the laity. The intellectual, in this case best represented by St Thomas Aquinas, was once again, typically, behind the times in going out of his way to display antagonism towards the most rapidly growing form of wealth which was trade. However, at least St Thomas was consistent. He was no growth enthusiast and would have rejected the modern assumption that time is money, for his thoughts dwelt on eternity. Indeed the ground on which he condemned usurers was that they were charging for time whereas time belongs to God.

With the Renaissance, the discovery of the new world and the resulting flow of precious metals to Europe, the Reformation and the coming of the spirit of nationalism, came a new style of economic thinking known as 'mercantilism'. In effect, mercantilism was the economics of Machiavelli. The supreme objective of the economic system was to advance the power of the nation state. This power was congealed as it were in silver and gold bullion. A country with no mines of its own could only acquire these precious metals, so mercantilists thought, by running a surplus on the balance of trade. For this purpose, since agricultural exports were not generally considered to be important, the vital aim was to expand exports of manufactures and minimise manufactured imports. This called for a highly interventionist type of government with general supervision of industry by state inspectors, bounties for exports and tariffs on imports. On the face of it mercantilism magnified the position of the trader too. Yet trade was not seen as a mutually advantageous exchange – but more like Clausewitz's conception of war, that is as an extension of policy. In terms of the new gospel of state power, it was industry that was really productive, trade that still carried with it the stigma of sterility.

The appearance of the French physiocrats of the mid-eighteenth century is generally considered to mark the beginnings of economics as a systematic study. Perhaps as a reaction against the luxury and extravagance of the French court, they, following Aristotle, would only allow that to be called wealth which derived from nature. That is to say agriculture was 'productive' and all other occupations were 'sterile'. This was at a time when commerce was developing on a scale unparalleled in Europe's history, and when manufacturing techniques advanced so fast that England, with France only just behind, was on the brink of her industrial revolution.

Adam Smith says in his *Wealth of Nations* (1776)[1] that the physiocrats) 'capital error' lay in their 'representing the class of artificers, manufacturers and merchants as altogether barren and unproductive'. However, he then himself classifies menial servants as among the barren and unproductive because their maintenance and employment is altogether at the expense of their masters and the work they perform is not of a nature to repay that expense. Such work consists of services which 'perish generally in the very instant of their performance and do not fix or realise themselves in any vendible commodity'. Equally barren, he thought, were some of 'the most

---

[1] Everyman edition, pp. 168, 169.

frivolous professions such as players, buffoons, musicians, opera singers', as well as some of the gravest and most important such as 'Churchmen, lawyers, physicians, and men of letters of all kinds'.[1] This distinction does not long bear examination. As McCulloch pointed out, Adam Smith's menial servant, who brought coal up from the householder's cellar was raising coal just as surely as the miner.

Ricardo did not think the function of the economist was enquiry into the causes of wealth or value as much as into the way the national wealth was distributed. Yet it was he who provided one of the bases of so called 'scientific socialism' with his labour theory of value. This amounted to the assertion that, taking utility for granted, and excepting a few cases like those of antiques and old masters where the issue is determined by scarcity, in the long run, and for the great bulk of commodities, exchange values reflect the amount of labour which enters into their production. Though in principle there was no reason why labour costs should not determine the values of services as much as of goods, the notion that labour was, so to speak, congealed in the product, fitted in better with the idea of tangible commodities than with services which perish in the very instant of their performance.

Jean Baptiste Say is best known as a populariser of the ideas of Adam Smith, but in his theory of value he improved upon his master. He rejected Smith's notion that immaterial products were not wealth because they were not 'susceptible of conservation'. He took the example of a doctor who cures a sick man. The patient at least would not agree that the doctor's labour was unproductive. He then asked if the doctor's product was capable of being exchanged. Certainly because the doctor's advice was exchanged against the fees, though the need for the advice ceased at the moment it was given. He thus argued that all activities which create utilities, that is, which have the satisfaction of the consumer as their first consequence, are productive. He therefore put agriculture, manufacturing and commerce on an exactly equal footing. At least, he did generally, for even Say had second thoughts about services. He did in fact accept Smith's view about immaterial products that they did not add to the national capital and consequently believed that there should not be too many of them. Yet who can now confidently assert with Smith and Say that

---

[1] Marshall later poked fun at the idea 'that a singer in an opera is unproductive, that the printer of the tickets of admission to the opera is productive; while the usher who shows people to their places is unproductive, unless he happens to sell programmes and then he is productive'. Alfred Marshall, *Principles of Economics*, op. cit., p. 67.

a song – for instance, the Beatles' 'Money Won't Buy Me Love' is not part of the national capital? Songs were certainly the main capital of the Beatles' former company 'Northern Sings'. Moreover, much as we might wish that some pop number might perish in the very instant of its performance (or better still before) we know from experience that once it has arrived in the top twenty it is fated to endure often beyond endurance.

The kind of unproductive service that Say most had in mind was that of lawyers endlessly piling legal complexity upon legal complexity. As a Frenchman born under the *ancien régime,* he wrote from bitter experience, for the courts at that time showed incredible skill in prolonging disputes. There was one notorious action between the tailors and the secondhand clothes dealers of Paris which lasted for three hunded years and was only terminated by the French Revolution.[1]

There was on this point something to be said for Say. He was arguing that lawyers were providing a service – the fostering of fruitless disputes – which the consumer did not really want. It could not therefore create any utility and was thus not real wealth. It was more of an indictment of the whole social order that it should allow some of its best talents to be frittered away on activities which the public did not even desire.

Adam Smith's confusion reappears in an interesting way in the works of John Stuart Mill, though the latter was raised on the teachings of Ricardo. For Mill production required a tangible result. Therefore only those utilities 'fixed and embodied in human beings' but not those 'consisting in a service rendered' could be said to issue from productive labour. Mill also, rather quaintly, applied the distinction to consumption. Thus an unproductive consumer was one who contributed nothing directly or indirectly to production. He gives an unwittingly comic description of a productive labourer going in for consumption which is unproductive because it did not result in 'keeping up or improving health, strength, capacities of work or in rearing other productive labourers' but instead concentrating on 'pleasures and luxuries'[2] Mill should perhaps have remembered the acid comment of Hume on luxury, that 'word of uncertain signification': 'To imagine that the gratifying of any sense, or the indulging of any delicacy in meat, drink or apparel is of itself a

---

[1] E.F. Heckscher, *Mercantilism,* trans. Shapiro, 2 vols, Allen & Unwin, 1956, Vol. I, p. 177.
[2] Quoted in W.E. Kuhn, *The Evolution of Economic Thought,* Chicago, South Western Publishing Co., p. 44.

vice, can never enter a head that is not disordered by the frenzies of enthusiasm.' One may indeed object that Mill was not concerned about vice, but the word 'unproductive' has strong overtones of moral condemnation.

In Marx, 'the Ricardian' labour theory of value becomes a full blown theory of exploitation. Labour is the source of value but the labouring class is largely deprived of its fruits by grasping capitalists and rentiers. However, for present purposes the point of interest is that Marx's 'value' is entirely materialist. He concerns himself exclusively with commodities. Services are not so much condemned as assumed to have no valid existence.

The consequences of many theoretical notions are obscure, but with Marx it is possible to point to cause and effect because, among the Communist countries, his works are treated as holy writ. It is not surprising therefore to find that in the Soviet Union, service activities are excluded from the national income because the authorities consider them unproductive. There result anomalies similar to those which arose in Great Britain following the introduction of the selective employment tax. As Alec Nove has put it in his book on *The Soviet Economy*[1]

> The present concept involves among other things, the idea that a railway signalman is productive when he lets a freight train past his signal-box but unproductive when he performs an identical function on the approach of a passenger train. Similarly a typist at a factory is productive, but the girl in Gosplan, who may type the letter in reply, is unproductive because a line has to be drawn between 'administration' and 'productive enterprises', and the two typists find themselves on opposite sides of the line.

If economists have underestimated the value of services, statisticians have helped to consolidate their errors.[2] The national income figures available have appeared to support the contention that the rate of productivity growth of services in both the United States and the United Kingdom postwar has been less rapid than that of manufacturing. We may leave aside the important considerations that the national output and employment statistics are formed into groups which are labelled either 'manufacturing' or 'services' but are in fact never purely the one or the other. The main point is that services have proved difficult to measure in terms of a price component and

---

[1] Allen & Unwin, 1961 (The Minerva Series no. 6), p. 22.
[2] See G.D.N. Worswick and C.G. Fane, 'Goods and services once again', *District Bank Review*, March 1967.

an output component. In particular the lack of a direct measure of services output has led the national income statisticians to resort to the use of employment as a proxy for output. Unfortunately this makes the resulting statistics useless as a guide to the service worker's productivity. For, if we divide the output indicator by the numbers employed, it appears that the productivity of labour is unchanged throughout. Worswick and Fane therefore conclude in their important study: 'There is a strong presumption that in most National Accounts statistics, the growth in the volume of services is understated and the corresponding implicit price deflators over-stated.'

If the method of compiling domestic statistics has tended to make services feel small, this is nothing compared to the extent to which, until recently, the balance of payments statistics strove to minimise them. The normal way of presenting the contribution of invisible exports (exports of services plus earnings in investment abroad) was to show them as a net figure, often, in the 1960s, of around +£150 million. Few realised until the publication of the Bland Report that even this net item was diminished by deducting from it the government's expenditure overseas. However, the comparative smallness of the sum led many otherwise well informed people, even among the economists, to believe that services were a far from vital part of Britain's trade. It comes as a shock to most of them even now to be told that invisibles represent nearly two-fifths of British exports. Indeed it is worth pointing out that, had visibles been treated in the same way as invisibles, the net achievement of British merchandise trade would appear as a regular annual deficit.

The undoubted prejudice against services found among many economists and politicians rests not only on dogma but also on a belief, at least in Britain, that the heyday of services is past because their glory belonged to the pre-1914 period of British commercial and financial supremacy. Services, especially financial services, are associated, particularly in the minds of the left, with the City, the symbol of capitalism and all its deplorable works. This belief in the declining importance of trade in services derives partly from memories of the changes which took place in the period 1914 to 1939, when under the impact first of war and then of depression, the liberal international economy in which British services had prospered collapsed. After recent balance of payments troubles it is chastening to recall that between 1911 and 1913, Britain was running an annual surplus of over £200 million on her balance of payments, all of which was invested abroad (equivalent to over £1000 million today).

The foregoing historical sketch set out to show how the myth of the non-productive character of services has grown up. That the myth's results have already been damaging is apparent to many businessmen who have had to contend with the now widely condemned British selective employment tax. This ill-starred fiscal innovation is an example of how a confusion of thought may lead to policies which are not merely irrational but are actively harmful to the economy. That the folly is not unique to Britain is shown by the Soviet Union, where, as we have seen, the national output statistics exclude services altogether. This in itself appears a harmless bit of statistical silliness which only affects official classifications. Unfortunately it affects policy, too. 'Unproductive' activities like distribution are sorely neglected. Indeed, Soviet Russia has about a quarter of the shops in relation to population possessed by the U.S.A. or Britain and those shops are understaffed and ill-equipped.[1] The burden of this deficiency falls on the Soviet citizen who spends many of his non-working hours in queues.

Marx's ideas must also have had much to do with the Soviet neglect of international trade. Even intrabloc trade was stagnant for many years after the war. Not until the death of Stalin did bloc politicians start thinking about mutual cooperation. 'Moreover, up to 1953–4, Bloc economic theoreticians completely neglected problems of foreign trade policy.'[2]

There is, however, a wider political issue. As has appeared from cursory references above to the ideas of J.K. Galbraith and Andrew Shonfield, the belief that large scale, concentrated industry, as opposed to small scale, dispersed services, provides the dominating influence on economy and society, leads naturally to a plea for more grandiose government to deal with this growth of private power. How validly can this plea be sustained in a predominantly service society? To this question we must now turn.

[1] L. Sire, *Economic Devolution in Eastern Europe*, Longman, 1969, pp. 35, 36.
[2] Frederic L. Pryor, *The Communist Foreign Trade System*, Allen & Unwin, 1963, p. 24.

3

The rise of the industrial state

Macaulay believed that the forces shaping his world were 'steam engines and democracy'. In more recent times we might change the formula to 'electricity and collectivism'. As Lenin said 'Communism is nothing but soviet rule plus electrification of the entire country'[1]

The common assumption now is that industrialisation promotes centralisation. Whose emphasis is right – Macaulay's or Lenin's? As regards the record of modern times certainly it is odds on Lenin. Since the beginning of this century world manufacturing output has risen roughly sixteen times: if an index of state activity were available it would probably have grown still more if only because of the rise of the bureaucratic Communist empires: there are actually ten million people engaged in making and administering the Soviet economic plan. The same trend towards big government has been apparent in the industrial countries of the West.[2] American federal government employment for instance rose twelve times between 1901 and 1970.

Everywhere there has been an advance of the central or federal authorities at the expense of private enterprise and local provincial or state authorities. This may assume the form of a simple takeover, as when the British government nationalised municipal and private bus services. It may be more indirect – as when the British local authorities become increasingly dependent for their revenues on the central government. However it occurs, the tendency for authority to gravitate to the central executive power is the same. Perhaps even more ominous is the tendency for the planning apparatus to bypass the institutions of democracy. In France the birthplace of indicative planning, and, subsequently in Britain, the secret 'dialogue' between civil servants and businessmen in the national planning councils was, until recently, showing every sign of displacing the public debate in the Chamber of Deputies or the House of Commons. If

[1] Speech of 21 November 1920.
[2] By 'big government' we mean government which is big both in scale and pretensions, employing a large bureaucracy and adopting an interventionist style of economic policy.

the collapse of the plan in both cases somewhat defeated the original intention it was for no want of trying among those principally engaged. In America there was complaint and with reason, about the 'government by guideline' which arrived with Kennedy and continued under Johnson. Kennedy, indeed, made no secret of his regard for the French planning system as a promising model for promoting US economic growth.[1] It was not only neurotic free enterprisers who saw in his Council of Economic Advisors an embryo Commissariat du Plan. If, happily, elections in France and the United States and less happily in Great Britain the sheer necessities of the debtor, slowed down the precipitous descent into collectivism, the generally widespread character of the movement admits of no complacency.

The issue must be faced by all serious students of western civilisation – whether this centralising trend should be resisted as the intimations of our democratic tradition would imply, or, as many leading intellectuals and most notably Galbraith and Shonfield have argued, it should be unreservedly welcomed. Must we indeed accept that the relevance of Jefferson, Burke and Mill are minimal in a technological age, accommodate ourselves to maxistyle government and, as Shakespeare's Cassius said of Caesar, 'Walk under his huge legs and peep about to find ourselves dishonourable graves'? Can it be that we genuinely have no alternative but resignedly to accept the technological imperatives requiring government which is not only powerful but discretionary as well?

The only rational answer can issue from an examination of those forces which have made the recent lurch towards Leviathan so pronounced. Inevitably this requires us to turn our attention to that prominent institutional form of modern enterprise – the corporation. There is need, if briefly, to recall the rather crucial point made in the previous chapter, that the large corporation's apparent dominance of the economy rests on a false impression created by certain economists who have greatly exaggerated the significance of the manufacturing sector, where it is prevalent, but which in the crucial American case comprises only about a quarter of total output. Even so it is the giant corporations which have made most impact on the public mind. It is the behaviour of these titans which most frequently leads to public outcry and leads through the normal democratic process of protest and counter protest, enquiry and rebuttal, to legislation and administrative action.

Among all the sins of private business none down the ages has

---

[1] Shonfield, *Modern Capitalism*, p. 74.

been better calculated to bring the government rushing in than the abuse of monopoly power. Not that governments were always so concerned to prevent the abuse as to profit from it. Thus in Tudor times monopoly was sometimes condemned as being against the general interest whereas at other times monopoly grants have been regarded as a valuable source of revenue. There are broadly two possible lines of state action. The first is to make laws against monopoly exploitation of the consumer which the courts must enforce. This is the traditional liberal solution where the enforcement of competition is seen as a central task of government. Only those who (often wilfully) misunderstand the rationale of a free enterprise economy refuse to recognise competition enforcement as a legitimate state function. Thus the endeavour to preserve the freedom of markets by constructing and maintaining a legal framework, or by the creation of an agency to this end, is frequently but wrong-headedly christened 'interventionsim'. Thus Mr Shonfield[1] cites the Securities and Exchange Commission in Washington, with its stringent standards of reporting of the affairs of companies, as an example of 'interventionism' in the United States. He admits that such government supervision is sometimes defended on the traditional grounds that it helps the market work properly but fails to mention how tradition errs. Likewise, the Conservative proposals for the reform of trades union law[2] met with the taunt that they involved the party which was opposed to controls in extending state intervention. Both these examples show how those who are hostile to the free enterprise system seek to define it as a suicidal economic order, prevented by its own blind doctrine of anarchic freedom for the entrepreneur from enforcing the principle of competition which gives it life.

The second, and unhappily far too frequent, response of government to monopoly is the attempt, invariably unsuccessful, to regulate its symptoms. Thus price control was the resort of the emperors Diocletian and Commodus as it was more recently with less crudity but no more success by Kennedy, Wilson and de Gaulle.[3] It is interesting that the hard sell for incomes policy has mostly been for its role in restraining powerful industrial or labour monopolies from raising wages and prices faster than productivity. The possibility,

[1] *Modern Capitalism*, p. 299.
[2] *Fair Deal at Work*, Conservative Political Centre, 1968.
[3] It is still too early to judge the success or failure of the price and income freezes of Nixon and Heath, but, in any case, they should only be judged as short-term expedients designed to change inflationary expectations, not as long-term solutions based on a reversion to collectivist thinking.

just as compatible with the empirical evidence in Great Britain at any rate, that the monopoly power might be incompetently exploited by the bumbling leadership of the large unions and thus actually slow down inflation, at least in its early stages, was generally ignored. The popularly accepted idea was that monopoly power must be at the root of inflation. It was generally accepted because, for a generation more, economics teaching, under the influence of a few extreme radicals who have specialised in the pure theory of monopoly, has greatly exaggerated its significance in the economies of western capitalism. Apparently this exaggeration also owed something to the importunities of publishers of economic textbooks who insisted that certain diagrams should be stretched for presentational purposes, thus magnifying the extent to which the monopolist plundered the consumer of his 'surplus'.

With informed opinion thus persuaded that monopoly was more prevalent than it actually was, there was no difficulty in convincing the less sophisticated mass that the economic order of which monopoly was typical must also be wicked. As Schumpeter put it: 'Economists, government agents, journalists and politicians obviously love the word because it has come to be a term of opprobrium which is sure to rouse the public's hostility against any interest so labelled.'[1] When the enemy is so generally disliked it is not unduly difficult to collect a lynching party. Monopoly power, or the power of the trusts, is a bogey which has served the needs of those seeking the expansion of state power very well. Not only is there a long tradition, in the Anglo-Saxon countries especially, of taming the power of over mighty subjects, but in the postwar period the recollection of how the Thyssens and the Krupps financed the rise of Hitler, has reinforced the popular dislike of concentrated industrial power. The activities of big business in democratic politics today are not, fortunately, so spectacular. In Britain, except for the occasional case of corruption in local government, the cruder forms of political influence by commercial interests are less apparent, though the most notable, which culminated in the Lynsky tribunal, involved one of Mr Attlee's junior ministers. In the United States the suborning of officials, and the bribery of legislatures is more general and undoubtedly more publicised. This has certainly helped to vilify business in the eyes of the public and provided collectivists from F. D. Roosevelt on with ample excuse for policies of hostile interventionism.

[1] Joseph A. Schumpeter, *Capitalism, Socialism and Democracy*, Allen & Unwin, 1965, p. 100.

However, policies of friendly interventionists has been even more fatal. Their origin is all too easy to understand. Big business failure means disaster writ large; shareholders lose their capital, workers lose their jobs and the government loses votes. Such were the circumstances which in the 1930s generated British protectionism. American new dealism and, in Germany, the perverse ingenuities of Dr Schacht. Yet perhaps there was no more startling example of how government salvage can lead to government control than in Mussolini's Italy. In the prewar slump the Fascist government encouraged the banks to support insolvent companies both by lending them money and by buying their shares. When bank shares in turn came under pressure they were encouraged to buy them too. Eventually this left the banks owning both themselves (so that in effect they were nationalised) and a controlling share of Italian industry. Thus began the IRI (Instituto per la Ricostruzione Industrale).

Italy's IRI is said to have provided the model for the late British Labour Government's creation IRC (Industrial Reorganisation Corporation). This was set up in 1966 to promote industrial rationalisation with the help of up to £150 million of Exchequer funds. Considerable claims have since been made for the achievements of the IRC in restructuring, indeed almost resurrecting, British industry Mr Harold Wilson has even suggested that the IRC was a major factor in the recovery in Britain's balance of payments in 1969. In fact, even making the assumption (for which experience so far provides scant support) that mergers promote efficiency, the IRC has only had dealings with a fraction of the total (though, admittedly, a spectacular fraction), and many of these would have occurred without its help. The claim that IRC's existence created a climate of opinion making mergers fashionable, is not even mildly convincing. For the most potent impulse to merge in the late 'sixties was provided by deflation, which reflected not purposive planning, but the hard-faced, hard line, hard money preferences of the Zurich gnomes. Only ideological unawareness or obtuseness can obscure the fact that the real potential of a body like IRC must be political rather than industrial. For, provided that nominees of the required political persuasion be put in charge, it might become an excellent contrivance for the extension of socialism. There could be loans for industrialists who toed the planners' line while recalcitrants could be squeezed out by government sponsored competition, mergers or takeovers.

Admittedly the IRC was only one of a number of the instruments of interventionism. The Industrial Expansion Act of 1968 added a further £200 million to the funds available to Labour ministers for their capricious incursions into industrial affairs. The Prices and Incomes Board again never had more than the most marginal impact on wages, prices or productivity: its chief function was to provide a respectable excuse for shelving, evading or delaying government decisions on awkward issues. Yet its nuisance value to firms, and especially the amount of valuable executive time it could waste compelled respect among industrialists who would otherwise have been inclined to treat it with the scorn which its economic futility invited. In its proposed reincarnation as the Commission for Industry and Manpower, when it was to have been merged with the Monopolies Commission, its ability to lean on all industrialists, who refused to conform to consensus thinking, would have been materially increased. It would have been able at will to hound with demands for the most searching financial information any business with more than £10 million of capital employed. With a little ingenuity of argument about the 'public interest' it could have justified price control according to its fancy thus imposing the most crippling limitations on any firm it chose and all in the sacred cause of preventing monopoly abuse. For the joy of it was that monopoly remained rather ill-defined. Happily Mr Heath does not intend to implement this scheme and the danger is at any rate postponed.[1] However, this baulked initiative does illustrate how even in an old democracy there can be no relaxation of the old vigil against the institutional risks of tyranny.

It hardly needs saying that the same logic by which the big corporation in the natural course of events stimulates greater government control is at work in the other corporate development, the cartel, which similarly attracts the intimate embrace of government. Indeed, that is what it is invariably intended to do. Once the message goes forth, as it always does when protectionist policies are in vogue, that privileges are to be had for the asking, there is a general convergence on the pork barrel. It is then the best organised who go away replete, namely the large concerns which tend to dominate trade associations. In any joint planning and any resulting deal with the government it is the big firm which rules the roost while the mavericks must conform or forfeit credits, investment grants or other sweeteners which are in the authorities' gift.

---

[1] The temporary Conservative support for such hapless concerns as Upper Clyde Shipbuilding should be seen not as a relapse into paternalism but as the tactical response of a government hard pressed by high unemployment and a dangerous level of industrial unrest.

The trend towards the corporate state which is emerging in this present phase of western capitalism is not easy to put into reverse. A rivalry is developing between big government and corporate bigness to assert ever more ambitious claims upon each other. Not merely do aggregations of corporate power provoke the state into enlarging its domain, the very process of intervention seems devoted to concentrating corporate power even more. Thus where there is a national plan, which on the Monnet principle emerges from the dialogue between industry and the state, convenience demands that industry's dialecticians be few. Naturally civil service mandarins share a greater affinity of outlook with big business bureaucrats than with the young Turks among the smaller new arrivals. So-called structural improvements which the government seeks in an industry will involve mergers. Thus, according to Shonfield, the members of the Commissariat du Plan

> talk among themselves in a kind of shorthand about an 80–20 ratio. They express their view that, to make effective planning possible, the distribution of output in industry ought preferably to be such that something close to 80 per cent of the production comes from 20 per cent of the firms. It is easier still to plan in this personal style if the number of significant firms in an industry is an even smaller proportion of the total. The planners are able to cope, after a fashion, with industries in which ownership is less concentrated but several of them seem to feel that a 60–40 relationship – i.e. 60 per cent of production in the hands of 40 per cent of the firms – would in the long run be unmanageable. . . . The planners make no secret of their belief in the iron law of oligarchy.[1]

It is clear from the foregoing that there are powerful forces stimulating the growth of both big business and big government. Yet it remains to be explained why so many intellectuals should welcome this development and seek only to speed it on its way. Why is it that the tradition formerly strong in Anglo Saxon countries at least, that individual freedom in economic as in other affairs, survives best where power is diffused, has become so weak?

The best answer seems to be that they have all been mesmerised by technology. Now that a man has been landed on the moon we must expect this technological idolatry to reach even more lunatic pro-

[1] *Modern Capitalism*, p. 138. There is another revealing anecdote on the same page about the way one of the officials checked statistics: 'He picked up a piece of paper which was lying on the table in front of us and having brought it to his nose sniffed it energetically: "One relies on one's sense of smell," he said. "There is nothing else to do."'

portions. Yet whatever the future holds the key argument currently is that which is put pithily by Professor Galbraith. 'Technology under all circumstances leads to planning; in its higher manifestation it may put the problems of planning beyond the reach of the industrial firm. Technological compulsions, and not ideology or political wile will require the firm to seek the help and protection of the state.'[1] It is evidently this technological element which is the 'new' element in what he calls the 'New Industrial State'. Yet the more one looks at the historical background, the more the novelty wears off. Like many other currently fashionable nostra this argument was a very popular one in the 1930s. For instance, Mr Lewis Mumford in his *Technics and Civilisation* said: 'As industry advances in modernisation a greater weight of political authority must develop outside than was necessary in the past.'[2] That is, as technology advances so state power must grow. Put thus baldly the proposition is not self evident. On the contrary the development of science on which technology depends is generally conceded to have begun in modern history with science's emancipation from political and ecclesiastical dictation. Scientific freedom broadly coincided with the arrival of constitutional government. Why, from the point of view of science, should some new absolutism be better than the old?

We are told that there is an extreme complexity about much modern technology requiring for its exploitation an array of expertise, especially in forward planning, a scale of research facilities, a size of organisation and a capital funds requirement which can only be provided by huge corporations in intimate association with the central government. Every one of these notions is contestable if we except certain activities like moon shots which have more in common with defence expenditure (one of its many justifications) than with the normal run of commercial developments. The general idea that a project, because it is complex, is best dealt with by centralised planning is at best a half truth. The biggest projects, the moon shot included, depend substantially on contracting out to small firms. Moreover the success of great enterprises rests very much on the ability of the Chairmen to delegate. Again the work of Professor Jewkes and others has shown that inventions are not by any means the sole preserve of the big research establishments, rather if anything the reverse, and that a rich diversity of sizes and types of research bodies is the surest formula for success. As for capital funds the belief that the government is the only supplier on

[1]Galbraith, *The New Industrial State*, p. 20.
[2]Lewis Mumford, *Technics and Civilisation*, Routledge, 1934, p. 420.

the scale required is sheer superstition based on uncritical acceptance of the propriety of present levels of taxation which eat into the natural source of private supplies of capital.

If the corporate state were really the best form of government for a technological age, it might be asked why, so far, it has realised itself most completely in some of the most backward countries – not only in prewar Italy and presentday Spain and Portugal, but in a number of South American countries, such as the Argentine. That country, at the end of Peron's reign, must have been one of the very few in the world where living standards were actually lower than they had been a generation before. It is surely not a complete coincidence that all these regimes tended to be corrupt, inefficient, bombastically authoritarian and intellectually philistine.

Nor was corporatism new even in its Fascist heyday. It was in essence then, as it is now, the economic philosophy of the *ancien régime,* which is generally considered to have reached its full flowering in the reign of Louis XIV under the administration of his gifted minister Colbert. According to the great authority on the subject[1] from the year 1666 until 1730 the regulations, mainly concerning textiles, filled four quarto volumes of 2,200 pages, and three supplementary volumes. These laid down in great detail the width of cloth and the equipment to be used. Ironically enough these complex directions were designed to guide workmen and even supervisors who frequently could not even read. How did Colbert know which methods to recommend? The answer is that, like the planners of today, he laid down as law what was already the practice of established manufacturers. This, it goes without saying, was a system implacably hostile to innovation. Thus the French Government did its best to protect textile producers against the competition of printed calicoes. The result, according to Heckscher was;

> It is estimated that the economic measures taken in this connection cost the lives of some 16,000 people, partly through executions and partly through armed affrays without reckoning the unknown but certainly much larger numbers of people who were sent to the galleys, or punished in other ways. On one occasion in Valence, 77 were sentenced to be hanged, 58 were to be broken on the wheel, 631 were sent to the galleys, one was set free and none were pardoned. But even this vigorous action did not help to attain the desired end.

The main result was that the French calico printing industry was

[1] Heckscher, *Mercantilism*, i, 157ff.

completely stunted in its growth. For after the 1686 prohibition the French craftsmen concerned emigrated to neighbouring countries.

If the ascendancy of the big corporation has been much oversold through the myopia and worse of publicists who have ignored all but the industrial sector where corporate power is entrenched, even its present eminence was not foreordained. Professor Galbraith himself admits at one point that it is not the technological imperatives which account for the vast scale of General Motors' operations. 'General Motors is not only large enough to afford the best size of automobile plant but is large enough to afford a dozen more of the best size.'[1] Yet his explanation that the size is necessary for business planning is seriously wanting. For planning is not an end in itself. The prime object of corporate planning is, on his own showing, growth. However, as Professor Allen has pointed out, this conflicts with the other Galbraith proposition that once corporations have achieved great size their security is assured. For, as he says, 'in practice the path of expansion pursued by one giant usually leads sooner or later into the territories of other giants and in this way established positions are constantly being challenged'.[2]

More convincing is the theory that great size in corporations is the product of corporate law. It is a human artifact as large as legislation allows it to be. The corporate dominions of Shell, Unilever and IBM are monuments to the creative power of limited liability. Unfortunately present arrangements in both Britain and America, notably the fact that one corporation is allowed to hold stock in another, offer scope for the operation of less constructive energies. It is essentially this provision which opens the door to mergers, the reduction of competition, and the building of huge, purely financial, structures.

In shaping the corporate environment the major factor other than corporation law is fiscal policy. The latter's importance was shown dramatically during the first takeover movement in Britain in the 1950s, led by Charles Clore, the property tycoon. For the takeover opportunities were created during the preceding period of dividend limitation and of corporation tax favouring retention of earnings. The most recent merger wave in the United States reflected the inequity of the tax burden as between debenture interest and equity earnings. It is true that limited liability status of some kind is inevitable if modern capitalist enterprise is not to be unreasonably restrained. Nevertheless it does not have to be limited quite in the

[1] *The New Industrial State*, p. 76.
[2] G.C. Allen, *Economic Fact and Fantasy*, IEA Occasional Paper no. 14, p. 21.

present way. Professor Hayek, for instance, has suggested that the holdings of corporations should carry no voting rights.[1] Others have urged imitation of the example set by West Germany where corporation tax discriminates against earnings retentions instead of in their favour. It would be possible for the law to compel a 100 per cent payment of corporate profits or, as Ralph Turvey has suggested, for tax to be levied on each shareholder's entitlement to corporate income whether paid out or not. This would encourage maximum distribution. Whatever their other merits all these measures would profoundly weaken the established positions of the industrial dinosaurs.

Professor Hayek argues further that it is the misdirection of corporate energies which leads to the growth of state control. The task of the corporation, he insists, is, while respecting the law and the ordinary decencies of human conduct, to make profits for the shareholders, nothing more and nothing less. He rejects the idea that the corporation management should increasingly reflect the public interest. On the contrary 'if the management is supposed to serve wider public interests, it becomes merely a logical consequence of this conception that the appointed representatives of the public interest should control the management'.[2] In this passage Professor Hayek is not making an academic point, but objecting to so called corporate philosophies popular in some managerial circles.

Typical of such corporatist views was a statement by Mr David Rockefeller when making his Chairman's statement to the Chase Manhattan Bank's annual meeting on 2 April 1970 when he said: 'We believe that our responsibility for human and social welfare must rank alongside our responsibility to maximise our return on our stockholders' investment.' Some managerial autocrats go further and claim not only that they are guided by a sense of social responsibility but that their superior moral attitude combined with their managerial expertise qualifies them as political rulers. The idea came into prominence among top British managers during one of the more disastrous periods of Mr Harold Wilson's government, when it was seriously suggested that Lord Robens, Chairman of the National Coal Board, should form a cabinet including business leaders and other top people to be called 'Great Britain Limited'.

If the corporate state works no fatal charm on, or rather, makes itself decidedly odious to, most of those raised in Anglo-Saxon

[1] F. A. Von Hayek, 'The corporation in modern society' in *Studies in Philosophy, Politics and Economics*, Routledge, 1967.
[2] *Ibid.*, p. 306.

libertarian tradition, do its practical advantages still offset its repulsiveness in principle? The usual defence of Mussolini was that even if he did use street violence as a method of government and forced his opponents to swallow castor oil, he also drained the Pontine marshes and made the trains run on time; that if he gassed defenceless Abyssinian tribesmen he nevertheless, like the Romans, whom he fancied himself succeeding, built roads. Even so, most dispassionate historians now agree that this classic corporate state was already a flop economically before it went down in ruin in the Second World War. The standard of living of the average Italian was falling throughout the 1930s, when in most countries it was recovering. This was partly due to the burden or armanents yet Italy was not even prepared for war, as the event was to prove.

It is, then, to more modern corporatist examples to which the advocate must turn. And he can scarcely avoid turning to Britain under its second Socialist government since the war. Yet here the evidence for him can be no more assuring. Growth under Mr Wilson was nearly halved compared with the previous six years despite unparalleled foreign loans and eventual devaluation.

This admittedly is a somewhat general and not necessarily conclusive criticism. More to the point is the performance of the nationalised industries which are surely the fulfilment of the corporate ideal, being avowedly run exclusively in the public interest. Yet, according to a study by George Polanyi, the British nationalised industries yield on average less than a third of the return of that in the private sector on capital investment whether this return be counted as growth of output or as profit. Indeed he alleges that if the public sector over the decade ending 1966 had been as productive as the private, Britain would have had an economic miracle comparable with those that took place on the Continent in the same period. He rebuts the objection that nationalised bodies should be judged by their social return to the whole community rather than their commercial return to the corporation. Social returns he argues, are non-measurable; cost-benefit analysis is little better than guesswork and anyway impossible to check after the investment has taken place. He remarks interestingly that one cannot assess what value people will place on a service, such as the provision of time-saving or increased comfort, through reduced road congestion, except by offering it to consumers at a price and finding out how much they are prepared to buy.'[1]

[1] George Polanyi, *Comparative returns from Investment in Nationalised Industries*, IEA Background Memorandum no. 1, p. 11.

A more recent study by D.R. Myddelton[1] showed that if depreciation took account of the inflated costs of replacing old capital then the average imputed losses for all nationalised industries (after charging interest) would be quadrupled, from about £60 million to £240 million a year.

R.W.S. Pryke has made a gallant and ingenious but unsuccessful attempt to challenge the nationalised industry productivity's ill repute.[2] He contends first that their labour productivity grew faster in the second ten years of nationalisation than in private manufacturing. On its own this claim amounts to little since it ignores the disproportionate amounts of capital injected into them to provide labour saving machinery etc. Other labour productivity gains in the coal industry, for example, resulted from the closing down of grossly inefficient pits. Even so the British coal industry is woefully unproductive by West German or Dutch standards.

In order to meet the objection that additional capital was bound to raise labour productivity Pryke attempted to measure the return on capital and labour combined. For private industry he took the total wage bill as the measure of the contribution of labour and profits to represent the contribution of capital. He then divided the sums of these into final output to find the output per composite unit of capital and labour. However, while he took actual wages his profit figure was the notional one of 10 per cent of estimated capital assets (10 per cent being the rate of return on manufacturing in the the best year, 1958). The object of using this imputed rate of profit was to avoid problems posed by losses which treated as capital inputs would perversely appear to result in higher productivity output. With these figures Mr Pryke demonstrates that 'Residual productivity', i.e. productivity of labour and capital industries, rose much faster in the nationalised industries than in manufacturing.

Unfortunately this method for all its adroitness is unreliable. For a start the 10 per cent rate of return arguably understates the capital contribution because it is based on the going rate in 1958, when capital was partly rationed by the Capital Issues Committee. Remove the rationing and let market forces assert themselves and the rate would have been higher. The importance of this point may be judged from the fact that rates of interest (the price of capital) doubled over the period of Mr Pryke's comparison. Yet the more any method of measuring the composite input of labour and capital

[1] V. Tanzi *et al.*, *Taxation: a radical approach*, Institute of Economic Affairs, 1970.
[2] 'Are the nationalised industries becoming more efficient?', *Moorgate and Wall Street Review*, Spring 1970.

understates the value of the capital contribution the nearer it comes to the pure comparison of labour productivity which is so misleading, especially when the admitted fault of the public sector is its wastage of capital resources. Even more methodologically damaging is the fact that labour imputs measured by wages paid are not independent of output. Thus, by the Pryke measure, objectively rising productivity when associated, as it normally would be in private business, with mounting wages, might show zero productivity growth. Looking at the other side of the coin a low wage policy in public industry associated with objectively stationary productivity could in the Pryke model exhibit rapid productivity growth. A method which can give such eccentric answers is worthless as evidence of the nationalised industries' economic performance. It is not altogether surprising if the progeny of the shotgun union of real wages with notional profits turns out to be an illegitimate productivity residual.

The most influential form of contemporary corporatism is undoubtedly French indicative planning. In overall results it was most impressive from 1959 to 1962 and it was at this time that it caught the imagination of journalists and business bureaucrats in Great Britain who, for their own reasons, had never responded to the still more impressive, longer continuing, and more solidly based miracle of Erhard's West Germany. Leave aside for the moment the dubious connection between indicative planning and French growth – M. Jacquest Rueff described French planners as 'like the cock who thought his crowing brought on the dawn'. Overlook the possibility that growth owed more to other factors such as devaluation or Marshall Aid or the adoption of some of M. Rueff's reforms of the economic structure and especially the removal of 'distortions' in pricing in important sectors.[1] Assume that the planners can take all the credit for the French miracle and still the case is not convincing. For it was too brittle. Despite all the ballyhoo about participation the French plan was an élitist affair run by a small and complacent group of technocrats. It was the Gaullist economy much more than the Gaullist political order which came crashing down when the students raised the banner of revolt. The explosion of popular discontent which ensued was the type of response which élitist government invariably invites, especially when that élitism takes the form of clamping down on wage increases (sometimes called 'having an incomes policy') which de Gaulle had done with some success

[1] For a more detailed treatment see the author's article 'France in the modern world', *Westminster Bank Review*, May 1966.

until the riots which made the franc's devaluation only a matter of time.[1]

Planning, like other earlier forms of corporatism, is essentially an inflexible form of economic government. There are, it is true, many who pin their hopes on plans which roll, readjust or change with every shift of circumstance. Yet these seem conveniently to forget that the strong suit of planning as it was first recommended was supposed to be the background of certainty which it gave to businessmen in forming their individual plans for expansion. The truth of the matter is that this claim was always something of a fraud. The most a government plan can do is to guarantee its own level of expenditure. Yet the adjustment of that, as British experience has shown, may have the most important role of all to play in reacting to short or medium term fluctuations in such vital areas as the balance of payments. Moreover, no plan can allow for the fact of surprise, unavoidable in a world of imperfect knowledge, whether that surprise arises from new discoveries or products, a revolution in popular tastes, or a natural disaster.

This chapter has concerned itself with industry because it is industrial experience, and even that selectively treated, which has provided the rationale of present-day collectivism. Clearly, if the experience, even in this sector where conditions appear to favour the big battalions, is far from conclusive in support of big government, how much more dubious must it be when applied, as it increasingly must be, to an economy in which conditions are often the reverse.

For it is in services that increasingly the consumer is expressing the individuality of his own personal wants, where controls and planning, necessarily conducted in terms of general categories and tending towards standardised products, are peculiarly inappropriate. The variety of services favours neither bigness nor concentration, but rather a corresponding divergence of size and diffusion of firms. Variety renders centralised planning increasingly futile and instead argues the need for growing responsiveness at the local and particular level. Thus it is not Lockeran or Jeffersonian sentimentalism which calls for a scaling down of government, it is the economic facts of life in the new service society.

---

[1]The impressive recovery of the French economy under M. Pompidou owes little or nothing to planning but a great deal to economy in public investment which has made room for a rapid growth of private saving and investment stimulated by inflation and aided by weak unions – *The Economist French Survey,* December 2, 1972.

4

White-collar revolution

It is a curious fact that the more hierarchical the society, the more social gradations tend to reflect themselves in different styles of dress. Thus Chaucer's pilgrims were all readily identifiable for what they were by what they wore. In America, the world's greatest democracy, even the President, by his dress, is indistinguishable from any other citizen. Economic advance tends to eliminate these outward and visible signs of social rank. Indeed, to judge by sartorial evidence, colour, romance and poverty are indissolubly linked, as the hippies of today seem bent on proving, with their combination of impoverishment and psychedelia. By the same logic it was the prosperous Victorians who, apparently following the opinion expressed by Mrs Gaskell in one of her novels – that men should always wear black – adopted the uniform, anonymous, democratic, black evening dress, which has been practically universal ever since.

The great economic and social transformation with which this book is concerned, is similarly linked with a change of clothing. The coming of the service society is signalised by a different style of neckwear. The blue-collar manual workers are yielding to a white-collared group consisting of four broad categories, namely clerical; professional and technical; managers, officials and proprietors, and sales. In 1957 the white-collar workers in the United States exceeded those with blue collars for the first time in history. The trend had been apparent for decades, though it accelerated in the postwar period. Until 1950 the growth reflected declines in employment in agriculture and mining while manual industrial workers still went on increasing their share. However, from 1950 on, the manual workers' share also started to decline. Between 1950 and 1968 the proportion of white collar workers in the total work force rose from 37.5 to 47.5 per cent (*Statistical Abstract of the United States,* 1968). The change has been worldwide and apparently inseparable from economic advance. In Germany, for instance, between 1882 and 1958 the ratio of white-collar workers to the total rose from 8 to 26 per cent while over the same period the blue-collar percentage remained at 50 per cent.[1] In Sweden between 1920 and 1960 the white-collar ratio rose from 11 to 35 per cent, while the blue collar ratio shrank from 70 to 51 per cent. In Japan between 1930 and 1963 among the non-farm workers the white-collar proportion rose from a tenth to over a quarter.[2]

Plainly this rise of the white-collar worker is closely connected with the expansion of services. That is not to say that all white-collar workers are employed in the service sector, though they bulk larger in that sector than elsewhere. Nor does it mean that all service workers are white-collar workers, certainly not on the wide definition of services which would include the work of dockers and dustmen. On the other hand, again, nor do white-collar workers only work in services though it is arguable that, the growing number of white-collar workers is not only attributable to the rapid expansion of the service sector in which they predominate, but to the increasing importance of white-collar activities in all the other sectors as well. This is admirably brought out in the Swedish statistics. These show that between 1930 and 1960 the proportion of white-collar workers increased in every field: In agriculture from 2 to 5 per cent, in industry from 9 to 23 per cent, in commerce and transport from 36 to 59 per cent, and in public administration and the professions from 29 to 58 per cent.[3]

Since 1950 the pattern of white-collar occupations in America has changed significantly. All the main groups have been growing, it is true, but at different rates. The clerical workers, though still the main group and continuing to represent over a third of the white-collar total, are being fast overhauled by that very varied assortment of people labelled 'professional and technical workers' which has jumped from 20 per cent to 29.5 per cent of the white collar total. Expansion was much slower among the other two main groups, namely salesmen and sales clerks, and managers officials and proprietors. Yet the scenario, which these figures suggest, is scarcely one to make a modern Marxist rejoice. For, here there is little support for any theory of a white-collar proletariat emerging to carry on the class struggle. Instead what presents itself is a spectacle of increasing variety of occupations with more and more people living by the sale of the their professional skills.

All the signs are indeed that the professional and technical group,

---

[1] Adolf Sturmthal, *White Collar Trade Unions*, University of Illinois Press, 1967, p. 372.
[2] *Ibid.*, p. 267.
[3] *Ibid.*

spurred on by technology and the onward march of the welfare state, will continue to thrive. However, it should not be long before the growth in the numbers of salesmen and clerks is arrested and even reversed by automation. There will be more supermarkets and fewer sales assistants. In time there will be universal computer storage and a sharp decline in paperwork. The latter development will be nothing less than the reversal of a trend which has been with us since Caxton. Narrowing our perspective to the last half century the move towards a more complex, more account and control conscious society, has meant, broadly speaking, the replacement of the Bob Cratchitt prototype with his high stool, his ledger and his quill pen, by a dolly secretary and a more calculating woman, namely the adding machine operator. This has been compatible with a great growth in clerkdom. For instance, in 1851 in Britain, clerks were only 0.8 per cent of the working population and female clerks were only 0.1 per cent of total clerks. A century later clerks were 10.5 per cent of all workers and three-fifths of their number were women. The white collar has thus been yielding to the plunging neckline. In the next stage of development with the increasing dominance of professional and technical groups of so called white-collar workers the symbol of the new class will, presumably be the sexless mortarboard.

Yet, seriously, it is very necessary to reject the widely accepted myth that the advance of technology will always favour the growth of unskilled workers. It is just as untrue of the service activities now as of industry in the past. The statistics suggest that, just as the demand for skilled work in industry has grown, not diminished, so the net result of office automation should be a shift towards a working force with a far larger number of people possessing professional qualifications. C. Wright Mills may have been right, when looking back from the early 1960s to argue that 'White-collar people have been pushed by twentieth-century facts towards the wage-worker type of collective economic life', for he was talking about the period in which the main body of white-collar workers – the clerks – were changing from a minority elite into a far less exclusive mass salariat. However, more recent trends, as we have seen, point in the opposite direction. Even so, sociological fact is one thing, the interpretation of it another. The great question is how the increasing number of white-collar workers will organise themselves. Can we expect in the new service society that trade unions will have the same importance as the old or will they decline with the reduced importance of industry as services come more and more to occupy the centre of the stage?

In fact there are striking variations in the amount of support which white-collar unions enjoy in different parts of the world. At first sight there seems to be a perverse relationship between the economic dominance of white-collar workers and the degree of their unionisation. Thus in many underdeveloped countries, the leading, if not the only, unions are those of the clerks. In Western Europe white-collar unions are generally overshadowed by their blue-collar brethren. However, it is in the United States, the first country in the world for the white collars to outnumber the blue, that 85 per cent of total union membership nevertheless consists of manual workers. Yet closer analysis does not support such glib generalisation. For instance, it is in Sweden, the richest European country, that the white-collar unions have achieved their greatest triumph, with prosperous Western Germany not far behind. The ups and downs of white-collar unions conform to no single facile explanation. The true position is more complex and also more interesting.

In the developing world the trade union is a comparatively recent phenomenon. Indonesia is an illuminating example. There, among the first unions to be formed, were those of customs officers and teachers in 1911, officials of the state pawn shops in 1913, employees of the state opium monopoly in 1916 and officials of the Treasury and Public Works Department in 1917.[1] This was typical of a pre-industrial society, mainly concerned with exporting primary crops, and raw materials, where the clerks in the docks, the railways, the shipping and the exporting offices, the teachers and government officials are the best; indeed the only, educated people. It is small wonder that they, the members of the community with greatest access to new ideas from abroad, rather than the illiterate coolies, or the peasant farmers, or even the usually militant class-conscious miners, should be the first to adopt a western institutional invention. It is not surprising either that the most politically conscious classes should embrace a movement which, though often socially repugnant, especially, for instance, to Brahmins, had the merit of being associated with anticolonialist sentiment in the metropolitan country. For those best qualified to rule their own country it was comforting to belong to a movement which was by its tradition the spearhead of working-class political aspirations and which flattered their ambitions while it assured them of their own exploitation.

At the other end of the spectrum, the unions, in the United States,

[1] W. Galerson, *Labour in Developing Countries*, University of California Press, 1962.

far from mouthing the rhetoric of exploitation, are, in general, ardent supporters of the capitalist order. It is amusing to recall the occasion when Samuel Gompers, greatest of America's 'Labour Statesmen' who served as Labour adviser to the Committee of National Defence during the First World War, went on a morale-boosting tour of unions in allied countries. Unfortunately the tour did not have the desired effect because he insisted on denouncing socialism wherever he went. As Dr Pelling has observed, America's trade unions seem to be more reconciled to American society than American society is to the unions.[1] It is tempting to see this as the result of some large social trend, say towards the bourgeois unification of the proletariat, for the United States in terms of its income structure, its social classlessness and its mass consumer patterns is the most middle class country in the world. However, the behavioural pattern of the American industrial worker in the steel, auto, rubber or textile and glass industries is middle-class too. This does not prevent him achieving high levels of union membership. The actual reason is more prosaic and organisational.

Professor B. C. Roberts[2] has argued that America's unions face a crisis of adaptation similar to that which faced them in the 1930s, when craft-dominated unions, with their high joining and subscription fees, and special attachment to the skilled worker were failing to meet the needs of the workers in the mass production industries. The failure was dramatised and the problem partly solved by a breakaway from the central body by a number of the more industrial unions led by John L. Lewis of the mineworkers, who incidentally, emphasised his disagreement by striking the leader of the carpenters on the chin. The result was the founding of the Congress of Industrial Organisations. The member unions of this new grouping, with fees low enough for unskilled workers to afford and spending on promotion on the lavish scale required for big recruitment, succeeded brilliantly in organising the assembly line workers of the new industries. The competition spurred the AFL to extend its recruiting among the unskilled. However, it seems that, following their success in the 1930s and '40s, a certain hardening of the arteries set in. As Professor Roberts puts it, the American unions now seem to regard white-collar employees simply as 'blue-collar employees with bleached shirts'. He quotes a speech of Everett Kassalow, Research Director of the Industrial Union Department of the now reconciled AFL – CIO:

[1] H. Pelling, *American Labour*, University of Chicago Press, 1960.
[2] In *Trade Unions in a Free Society*, Hutchinson for IEA, 1962.

In the United States it will not be possible to choose the road of building separate professional and technical unions for many of these workers. Economic power in America, to a considerable extent, flows along corporate and industrial lines. If white-collar professional and technical workers are to be effectively organised they must somehow be grouped together in the great institution which industrial workers have already established to offset the great centres of corporate power – namely the powerful industrial unions in steel, auto, rubber, oil textile and other fields.[1]

Mr Kassalow then went on to point to where several AFL – CLO affiliates had already managed to organise large numbers of white-collar and professional workers, including the Communication Workers of America, the Airline Pilots and the American Radio Association.

These examples are revealing because they refer to the least typical service industries where economic power does indeed flow along corporate and, in a less precise sense, industrial lines. Unfortunately the wish appears to be father to the thought. If economic power really did flow along corporate, not to mention industrial lines, the prospects for American trade unions would be fair indeed. For the organisation men who run the corporations have long ago abandoned the hostility to unions so common among their entrepreneurial predecessors. On the contrary they tend to embrace the unions as agencies ideally qualified to promote the gospel of belongingness. In terms of modern management philosophy, unions should be instruments of 'governance' rather than instruments of war.

However, as has been shown earlier, the most representative service activities are those which are least subject to the dominance of the corporation. Plainly, then, for as long as the policy of American Unions continues to be based on the myth of corporate hegemony so eloquently stated by Mr Kassalow, for so long will they fail to establish themselves in the most promising field for recruitment.

Nevertheless, one cannot put the whole blame on America's union leadership for the failure to meet the challenge of the white-collar revolution. Still more important have been the peculiar circumstances of American historical development which have created a public opinion and in consequence a political and legal framework far less favourable to the unions than in most other western countries. It is difficult to overestimate the influence exerted by the frontier. It must have lured away many energetic spirits who, had

[1] *Ibid.*, p. 111.

they stayed, might have become the spokesmen of working-class discontents, and the natural sources of union activity and leadership. More intangible, but no less influential has been the fact that trade unions consort ill with the tradition of rugged individualism which was indeed characteristic of frontier society but which still survives nearly a century after the actual physical frontier has disappeared.

If, to many native born Americans, unions were either unnecessary or alien, to the hordes of immigrants who came in the generation before the 1914–18 war they appeared in a still less attractive light. Often the unions seemed to be exclusive bodies concerned mainly to further the interests of American born workers and very likely at their expense. The immigrants, most of whom were not familiar either with the English language or with trade union practice, and whose overriding interest was in obtaining work rather than extending workers' rights, did not make ideal union material. Nor was the situation helped by the frequent use of immigrant labour by anti-union employers to break strikes. Thus, at a time when in many other countries the trades unions were consolidating their position, in America they were still absorbed in the difficult task of digesting huge numbers of first or second generation immigrants.

It is no wonder then that American public opinion has often been unfriendly to trade unions and that politically they have had a much less easy ride than in many other western countries. The failure of the unions to achieve social and political respectability has made it particularly difficult for them to be accepted by the middle class, and consequently to recruit the essentially middle-class white-collar worker. During most of the century indeed, the unions have been on the defensive against legislative and judical action. They were harried under the Sherman Anti-trust Act of 1890 as combinations in restraint of trade. The Clayton Act of 1914, which appeared to exempt them, became by judical interpretation a restraint on the unions' power to call strikes and set up pickets. The best period for the unions arrived with Roosevelt's New Deal, under which the policy was to encourage trade unionism in the hope that workers' resistance would slow down the spiral of deflation. The Wagner Act of 1935 protected the worker's right to organise and bargain collectively and forbade any coercion of the worker to join an employer-dominated organisation. The Second World War, though it led to increased recruiting, saw grave damage done to the unions' image owing to the high incidence of strikes at a time of national danger and mounting concern about the growing influence of the Communists in their ranks.

The wave of strikes after the war increased the alienation of public opinion. This prompted legislation, most notably the Taft Hartley Act of 1947 which so greatly diminished the privileges which the Wagner Act had conferred on them that the unions described it as a 'Slave Labour Act'. In the present context, though, perhaps the most significant feature of the Taft Hartley amendments was the provision that no bargaining unit including higher foremen or supervisors could be set up by the Labour Relations Board. This may prove a serious handicap to the development of white-collar unionism in the USA if these high status employees are denied the collective bargaining rights which the mass of other workers enjoy. The unions continued to be on the defensive against state legislation during the 1950s and the McClellan congressional hearings with their serious revelations of corruption in the Teamsters' Union under the notorious James Hoffa's leadership led to the so-called 'Hoffa's Act' in 1959, which laid further restrictions on such matters as union elections and finances. However, the picture is not entirely discouraging from the union point of view. A presidential order in 1962 marked a shift in the government's attitude to federal employees from the past one of mere tolerance to positive encouragement of union membership. In this case, therefore, white-collar unionism is working with the tide, for it is allied to Parkinson's law.

Nevertheless, the story of America's unions in the white-collar field is one of failure. Is this really a result of conditions peculiar to America, as we have tended to argue, or is this failure in the country with the world's largest group of white-collar workers the pattern for the future and inherent in the nature of the service society? Experience in Europe surely suggests that this is not so. For there, though the service sectors are not so large, white-collar recruitment has prospered in many countries. This fact, at least, suggests that there is no compelling sociological reason why white-collar workers should be less capable of unionisation than their blue-collared brethren, though in the literature of trade unionism such glib sociological generalisations abound.

Fortunately the scholarly study of Mr G. S. Bain, *The Growth of White-Collar Unionism* (Oxford University Press, 1970) enables us to dismiss the bulk of them. He starts from the fact that in Great Britain the degree of unionisation among white-collar workers at 29 per cent (in 1964) was considerably less than the 51 per cent among manual workers. He then makes a careful statistical examination of many of the alleged causes for this differential. He concludes that there is no significant relationship between the growth of white-collar unionism and (*a*) such sociodemographic characteristics of white-collar workers as their sex, social origins, age and status; (*b*) such aspects of their economic position as earnings, other terms of conditions of employment, and employment security; (*c*) such aspects of their work situation as the opportunities for promotion, the extent of mechanisation and automation and the degree of proximity to unionised manual workers; (*d*) such aspects of trades unions as their public image recruitment policies and structures. He finds, however, that white-collar unionism is significantly related to employment concentration, union recognition and government action. The only positive independent sociological factor is thus employment concentration. The most highly unionised white-collar groups are the draughtsmen and journalists, both groups being concentrated in large establishments, indeed, in the latter case, to a considerable degree in one street. Bain observes that concentration means more bureaucracy, that individual white-collar workers feel increasingly unable to exert any influence on the making and administration of the rules which govern their jobs, and that it is to protect themselves against this that they join unions. He concludes that increasing concentration will favour the growth of white-collar unions but that this tendency itself will depend very much on extending employer recognition, which in turn will be mainly influenced by government action. Considering that Bain's evidence is largely based on statistics from the manufacturing sector – where as we have seen, concentration is more marked, but which is also of diminishing importance – the indications are that the one autonomous sociological influence, namely concentration, is itself exaggerated. The conclusion must be that the political climate is of overriding importance. Whether white-collar unions flourish or not seems to be largely a question of whether or not politicians pass laws and administrations act in helpful ways.

For instance, in Great Britain after the publication in 1918 of the Whitley Committee report it became official government policy to encourage union recognition throughout the economy. The encouragement applied directly to all in government employment. Union recognition has since become automatic in the civil service and all state establishments. White-collar unionisation has consequently become far more complete in the public than the private sector. It is thus not without some consideration of their own interests that British trade unions have consistently supported nationalisation. For the larger the public sector the greater union membership tends to be. Socialism indeed favours trade union growth. It is no coincidence that Sweden with 70 per cent unionisation among her white-collar workers has had forty years of socialist government. In France again the civil service is the only well unionised sector of the economy with 40 per cent of potential membership compared with only 20 per cent in private industry. It is illuminating, too, that the leadership of the French white-collar unions which was traditionally found in the *grands magasins* has shifted to the nationalised banks and insurance companies.

We should not neglect either the effect on the psychology of the middle-class white-collar worker of the government in power being socialist. 'Power', as Napoleon said, 'is never ridiculous.' More than that, with time it usually tends to become respectable. In Britain many trade union leaders have become cabinet ministers and rounded off their careers in the House of Lords. Such intimacy with the centres of decision has had a chastening effect on the British union leaders, too, who have gone to considerable lengths to root out Communist influences in their ranks. As a result British middle-class people more often regard the trade unions as stodgy rather than dangerous. Perhaps this is why major white-collar unions have been joining the Trades Union Congress in recent years, the most notable successes being the National and Local Government Officers (NALGO) in 1964 and the National Union of Teachers in 1970.

This is not to say that no strains exist. The old resentments recur. The manual worker's jealousy of the office worker with his clean job, his shorter hours and longer holidays, his separate canteen and other privileges, still survives below the surface. It occasionally comes to the boil, as for instance in the speech of Mr John Boyd at the TUC annual conference in September 1966. It was the more significant because Mr Boyd of the Amalgamated Engineering Union was, that year, none other than the Chairman of the National Executive of the Labour Party. Naturally enough in the circumstances he was on this occasion defending the Labour Party's proposals for a tougher compulsory incomes policy against the arguments of the two white-collar unions NALGO and ASSET (Association of Supervisory Staffs, Executives and Technicians) which opposed the policy. He started by accusing NALGO members of enjoying, as compared with manual workers, greater security, longer holidays, better superannuation and better sick schemes. Yet, he went on, 'you represent people who produce nothing'. He then turned on Mr Clive Jenkins (then leader of ASSET), and called him an anachronism because he represents people who have run away from the struggle of the workshop floor, who do not want to be associated with manual workers' unions so they join this whatever-you-call-it. In fact the vast majority of his people are people who have betrayed the manual workers' union – [cries of dissent] – and in my opinion they are 40,000 Conservatives run by half a dozen Clive Jenkinses [interruptions].

Still more disconcerting than this outburst, which might after all be discounted as the product of hyper-excitement at conference time, is the tale of the struggle for white-collar recognition in the British Steel industry. This arose after nationalisation because there were many unorganised white-collar workers, previously members of company staff associations, who were now encouraged to join a union. Not unnaturally they mostly chose the white-collar unions, namely the Clerical and Administrative Workers Union (CAWU) and the Association of Scientific, Technical and Managerial Staffs (ASTMS, led by Mr Clive Jenkins since 1968).

However, these unions were not represented on the trade union consultative committee for the steel industry which the TUC had set up before vesting day. In order to further their case the white-collar unions brought out on strike their members in the motor as well as the steel industry. The British Steel Corporation referred the dispute to an impartial commission chaired by Lord Pearson, which reported in favour of recognising the white-collar unions. At this the sixteen manual workers' unions threatened strike action so the TUC General Council stepped in as mediator. Its conclusions were so blatantly biased against their interests that the white collar unions dismissed them as 'a surrender to gangsterism'. The main findings were, first, that the bargaining rights of the two unions should be kept to their limited local level of July 1967, before the vesting day of the British Steel Corporations, that is the white-collar unions were to be limited in future to local negotiations; secondly it took the opportunity to assault the position of a third white-collar union (the Steel Industry Management Association) by ruling that it had no right to negotiate for workers below departmental managers. Finally it urged that there should be no further enquiry into the white-collar claims until the Steel Corporation and the TUC's Steel Committee (all manual unions) should agree.

Why was there such a bias against the white-collar unions? Mr Ian Mikardo, vice-president of the ASTMS, suggested the most compelling reason – that, of thirty-eight members of the TUC

General Council, sixteen were members of unions which were parties to the dispute, but there was no member of his union or that of the clerks of the CAWU.

Such conflicts prompt the questions: Is it better for white-collar unions to have their own separate congress? Is white-collar apartheid likely to lead to more union recruitment of white-collar workers? In Western Germany the division does exist and seems mainly to reflect a settled belief among the white-collar workers in their superior status. The members of the Christian Democrat trade union of clerks (DHV) indeed regard themselves as 'co-workers' with the management, naturally enjoying precedence over their horny-handed compatriots. It is arguable that this exclusive attitude is already outmoded and that white- and blue-collar workers are nowadays affected to much the same extent by rationalisation and automation. Yet these class distinctions often run deep and correspond not only to established ways of thinking but are still often as in the Austrian case embedded in wage and social legislation.

Nor is this all, for there is the question of political allegiance. The affiliation of the TUC with the Labour party in Britain has certainly deterred some white-collar unions from joining. In Sweden the manual workers confederation, LO, is similarly affiliated to the Social Democratic Party, but this raises no difficulties because the white-collar workers have their own central body TCO, which is politically neutral. The West German Clerks Union, DHV, is fervently Christian Democrat and explicitly opposed to a Socialistic economic order.

The white-collar tide can scarcely fail to envelop the politics of all economically advanced countries. In the United States, for instance, unless the trade union movement has considerably greater success in recruiting them than in the past, the proportion of America's workers which is at least unionised will shrink and the political weight of the unions will diminish correspondingly. The obvious gainer should be the Republican Party for, ever since the days of Roosevelt's New Deal, the American unions have habitually dwelt in the Democratic camp. Alternatively the white-collar workers of America might become more unionised. Assuming that the trade unions' central organisation does not at the same time split in two – as the challenge of recruiting industrial workers into a mainly craft-based movement divided it in the 1930s – by the 1980s there could be a trade union movement with more Republican inclinations.

The general impression is certainly that white-collar sympathies are frequently attached to the parties of the right. As we have seen the West German clerks are wholeheartedly Christian Democrat. In France the stronghold of the Catholic unions is among the white-collar workers in private industry. In Britain many white-collar unions have avoided affiliation to the TUC, or affiliated only with reluctance, because of the TUC's close links with the Labour Party.

Is the lesson of all this that the proletariat is becoming gradually more bourgeois as the white-collar working force grows and are the politics of the Western democracies, destined as a result to become increasingly middle-class and conservative? If that seems the most obvious reading of present trends there is at least one interesting sociological argument to the contrary. This is put forward by David Butler and Ronald Stokes in their book *Political Change in Britain* (Macmillan, 1969). Here, with qualifications, they assert that the trend is towards a permanent Labour majority. This thesis rests on the observation that there has been a growth in the number of Labour fathers, that there tends to be a strong hereditary element in voting, and that Labour fathers are given to having more children. The weakness of this theory is that it is little more than an aspect of the fact that the Labour Party has grown from almost nothing over the last half century to its present position as one of the two major parties in the state, for it is hard to see how any party can grow without including more fathers except in the unlikely case of a party consisting entirely of celibates. Nor is the discovery that fathers of working-class parties are more fertile or at least less assiduous about birth control exactly earthshaking. However, one of the tables in Butler and Stokes's book suggests a different conclusion from the one they have drawn. It is as follows:

Support for Labour among union and non-union
families by occupational grade, 1964

	Supervisory Non-Manual III	Lower Non-Manual IV	Skilled Manual V	Non-skilled Manual VI
Proportion voting Labour:	%	%	%	%
Among union families	42	56	72	78
Among non-union families	18	20	53	62

Since the non-manual workers are fated to outnumber the manual ones, the implication of this table would seem to be that Labour's position is deteriorating. It certainly seems as legitimate to assume that the above tendency for support for Labour to fall with the rise in occupational grade will continue in future as to assume with Butler and Stokes that the hereditary factor in voting behaviour will be as constant in future as it has been in the past. It is a matter of undisputed fact that the Conservatives manage to win elections more often than their opponents by collecting the bulk of the middle-class vote and around a third of the more numerous vote of the working class. One interesting suggestion by Glazer is that the middle-class Labour voters are those who belong to the 'helping professions' such as Welfare work, because they have become more socially conscious and reformist in their attitudes. John Raynor, in his book *The Middle Class* (Longmans, 1967) suggests that, following Glass, the increasing number of young people obtaining university education and studying social sciences or doing social work may mean more middle-class radicals. However, one could equally argue from this kind of evidence that radical Labour sympathisers in the middle classes are those who work for state welfare organisations, that they are voting less on behalf of social consciences and more on behalf of their jobs or anyway in support of the party which wants to expand their department. This is indeed how socialism creates socialists. It is interesting to note that in France it is in the civil service and the nationalised industries that the left wing unions find their most ardent white-collar support.

If middle-class loyalties really are being lured by state-owned agencies towards socialism the instinct of electoral self-preservation will no doubt reinforce the intimations of doctrine and lead even the most pragmatic Tory administration to restore the offending agencies to private ownership. It is perhaps not surprising that the belief, as widespread as it is erroneous, that the economies of advanced countries consist overwhelmingly of manufacturing, usually on a large scale, has been the launching pad for further errors of doctrine concerning labour relations, or 'industrial relations' the phrase used in Britain, which itself enshrines the fallacy.

Many of those who wish to reform the British trade union structure, for instance, often see the American pattern as the ideal, and contrast the classic monolithic authority of Walter Reuther's United Automobile Workers with the chaos of occupational jurisdictions within the British Motor Industry. Yet as we have seen it is precisely the CIO Industrial Union pattern which is best calculated to alienate the growing body of white-collar workers in the United States. Federalism and the development of the general union among British workers have in fact made it possible to carry on industrywide bargaining without adopting the admittedly much tidier industrial style of trades union. This has not only reduced the institutional barrier to the recruitment of white-collar workers but has avoided much interunion conflict. As Professor B.C. Roberts has pointed out, the single outstanding example of an industrial union, the National Union of Railwaymen, is an unfortunate one. The NUR was established as a deliberate exercise in the theory of scientific union organisation and meant to be the 'new model', the crowning achievement of the industrial union movement. Yet in this case there has been the most bitter history of interunion conflict.

Nor is it certain that the productivity bargaining so characteristic of America's industrial unions, and the object of much ecstatic praise, is so unmixed a benefit as the experts have asserted. In a typical encomium Andrew Shonfield paid a glowing tribute to the system in his influential book *British Economic Policy Since the War* (Penguin Special, 1958). He said of the United Automobile Workers and the United Steel Workers of America:

> Such unions start their negotiations with the explicit demand on the employers that they must do whatever is necessary – by way of investments and improvements in organisation – to increase output per man by a substantial annual amount in the two or three years ahead during which the wage contract is to run. They now take the adjustments for *future* productivity just as much for granted as the automatic adjustments to current changes on the cost of living sliding scale. But of course, in making these techno-logical demands on their employers, they have to be ready to accept radical alterations in plant and methods and dismissal of workers if these become redundant as a result of improved methods of output (p.20).

This is a characteristically idyllic British account of America's industrial unionism, in which militancy for once is virtuous because allied to the sacred pursuit of productivity – the holy grail of current policy endeavours. He even goes on to quote approvingly an 'en-gagingly frank' description by Nat Weinberg of the United Automo-bile Workers of the method of bargaining employed by his union, which is well calculated to drive some weaker firms in the industry out of business altogether. In fact this bullying technique, especially when employed by a major union against small firms, has aroused much criticism in the United States in the case of the notorious

Teamsters union. The apologetics should not be allowed to disguise the fact that this is an example of the abuse of dominant market power which is not tolerable in a free society.

To return to the main point about productivity bargaining: to the extent that the increase of wages is tantamount to a bribe to the workers to drop labour restrictions, a mutually satisfactory bargain which is not inflationary should be possible. However, if the increased productivity results from a combination of reduced labour restrictions plus more capital investment the consequence may well be inflationary, for the idea that management will be stimulated to prodigies of increased efficiency and modernisation by the sheer exorbitance of trades union demands is based on little more than optimism. It is the nature of management to be always searching for improvements. It is positively Panglossian to believe that some sudden enlightenment will descend on managers, a new vision of the state of the managerial art, as a sudden consequence of their being exposed to extortion. This theory of progress, through shock revelation, is not by the way confined to the American scene. It was the basic article of belief of Aubrey Jones and his staff on the British Prices and Incomes Board. In handing down his decision on some pay dispute, it was common form for Mr Jones to instruct the industry concerned that some part of the rise in wage costs could be absorbed by increased productivity which, it was implied, was there for the taking, simply because he, like Moses, had pronounced and they, like errant Israelites, had but to hear in order to know that it was good.

So, not only was the vaunted increase in productivity quite likely to be illusory, but the effect on the growth of the American economy may have been extremely harmful. Let us begin with the overall statistical position.

According to Victor R. Fuchs's analysis, service employment between 1929 and 1965 grew 0.9 per cent faster per year than industrial employment, but none of this increase could be explained by a shift of final output of services. Fuchs attributes 0.4 percentage of the difference points to a faster decline of hours in services. For the 0.4 or 0.5 percentage points of difference he gives the credit to a faster rate of technological change in industry and to the greater economies 'of scale reaped in that sector'. However, it seems likely that capital investment is essential in order to realise both the boons of technology and the extra economies of scale. If this is so, then it remains to be explained why industry should have attracted more investment than services. The likely answer is, first, that the trade unions which are concentrated in the industry sector have succeeded, by their high wage demands, in stimulating labour-saving investment to a greater extent than in the services where the unions are weak. Second, the large corporate organisation, which is more typical of industry than services, has found it easier to acquire the funds for capital investment.[1] This is because the large corporation has privileged access to the capital market: its size gives it higher credit standing, so it is able to borrow more money at less expense. Yet, this advantage of scale in borrowing funds has little to do with the real merits of the investment potential of industry as opposed to services. It is at least possible that productivity bargaining between the militant industrial unions and the large industrial corporations of America has effected a gigantic misallocation of American capital resources. This would go far to account for the relatively disappointing growth of the American economy in the 1950s and '60s. In the decade 1960–1970. US annual growth per person employed at 2.7 per cent was lower than that of both the European Community (4.3 per cent) and of every single one of the EFTA countries except Britain. Paradoxically the very feature of US trade union behaviour which is usually considered just cause for national pride, and is the object of general admiration in countries abroad, may in reality prove to be the American economy's Achilles heel.

Another example of how the prevalent belief that the economy is overwhelmingly industrial darkens counsel is the rise of incomes policies among the nations of the West. The problem to which these were offered as a solution, was the notorious one of reconciling Keynesian full employment policies with stable prices. It became all the more difficult as growth mania developed after the launching of the first sputnik, when the Western nations began to fear– groundlessly as it turned out – that they would be overtaken economically by the Soviet bloc and sought, by means of indicative planning and other forms of state action, to promote economic growth. This only added fuel to the flames of inflation. As usual one form of intervention justified resort to another. It was argued that if inflation was to be avoided without sacrificing other desirable aims, general restraints like monetary policy were ruled out because they would cause a politically unacceptable rise in the level of unemployment. It was here that the industry model came into play. For, it was said, the

---

[1] There is some support for this theory in a sample of ten industries in the USA comparing rates of capital-embodied technological growth that the motor vehicle industry took first place. If steel had been included it would have been high up too. See Edwin Mansfield, *The Economics of Technological Change* (Longman, 1969), p. 31.

villain of the piece was collective bargaining at a national level between big industrywide trade unions and employers' associations. Since it applied to all producers alike any increase could be added to selling prices with impunity. This added to everyone else's cost of living and therefore prompted other wage demands which would keep the spiral of prices and wages moving merrily skywards. This, in a nutshell, was what was known as 'cost-push' inflation. The implication was clear and was clearly drawn by the OECD in its report *The Problem of Rising Prices* in 1961. It put the ultimate blame, especially in the British case, on key bargains, which were then generalised. The OECD prescription was for the state to intervene to limit the magnitude of these wage increases, and keep them within some norm or guideline based on the predicted productivity growth of the whole economy.

This policy at the time looked harmless enough even to many free market supporters, because the degree of state intervention (which applied only to key bargains) was thought to be minimal and could even be presented as a form of antimonopoly policy with the state acting appropriately in a free enterprise economy, to restrain the abuse of dominant market power. Few appreciated at the time that so far as a free economy was concerned, the analysis only gave support for sporadic interventionism to affect short-term price movements. The idea that the whole economy could be tuned through a few crucial wage negotiations could not possibly provide the basis of a long-term policy. It overlooked the fact that bargains subject to persistent interference would cease to be key bargains. Logically therefore, a long-term imcomes policy could only lead to a regime of comprehensive price and wage control. Nor is it even now certain that the more publicised wage negotiations of certain blue-collar workers are any more significant than any others. It is interesting that a study in July 1968 published in Oxford Economic Papers, by V. Argy, of the University of Sydney, came to the tentative conclusion that trade unions in the United Kingdom have not behaved aggressively, that is, have not generated an excessive amount of cost inflation compared with other countries.[1] The OECD's earlier singling out of the UK as a striking example of cost-push inflation generated by the militancy of a few big unions looks rather insecure. Indeed it would be generally conceded that the big British so-called 'Key bargain' unions, like the Transport and General Workers

[1] It is, however, arguable that since 1968, with the help of higher redundancy payments and higher social benefits for strikers, cost push has finally come to stay in Britain: See G. Habesles, *Unions and Inflation*, I.E.A., 1972.

Union, are less efficient and less intelligent about exploiting their market power than small and better led unions such as the Association of Supervisory Staffs Executives and Technicians. In the present state of knowledge, indeed, it seems possible to hold the exactly opposite view to the original OECD report and infer that the big unions, by their restraint, had in fact tended to damp down inflation rather than add fuel to its flames. In any event, whatever the final verdict on the economic utility of incomes policy as a method for quelling inflation, its key political importance is as an instrument for the concentration of power. Indeed, the classic apologists for a wages policy[1] and their present intellectual heirs have all along been primarily interested in using government coercion for the purpose of creating a society with greater equality of incomes. Thus the controversy over incomes policy may appear to be only an academic dispute between, those favouring a cost-push theory on the one side and demand-pull enthusiasts on the other. Yet the important divide for policy purposes is between the collectivists who wish to politicise incomes and the libertarians who want incomes to remain primarily a matter of voluntary agreement between free contracting parties. Naturally, those who wish to subject incomes to centralised direction by politicians, are attracted by the Galbraithian picture of an economy dominated by big industry and big unions. In the first place, the idea that wages or anything else should be settled by a duel between those monsters is indefensible as part either of a rational economic order or as part of a democratic political order where such power concentrations are plainly dangerous to personal freedom. Yet this concentration makes the system all the easier to bring under central control. The system can, with little adjustment, be made to conform with collectivist goals. To Professor Galbaith the big union is 'an important factor in planning', and its role in Western economies has in recent times increasingly, and in his view rightly, approximated to that of the trade unions in Soviet countries.

It is indeed only by rejecting the myth of the industrial state that it is possible to reinstate the unions as necessary institutions in a free economic order. Amid the increasing variety and power of the service society trade unions too must become more like service centres and less like industrial cartels.

Ideally, in wage determination, union size should not matter as long as the wage bargain is carried on at the firm level and as long as the big trade union does not use its size to victimise the small

[1]See, for example, Lady Wootton, *The Social Foundations of Wage Policy*, Unwin University Books, 1955.

concern. For that is the way to escalate the conflict up to the national level and to invite centralised interference yet again. It is better to allow the wage bargains to be localised while the expertise provided, on the one hand by the trade union, and on the other by the trade association, arrives in each case from headquarters.

Collective bargaining, though the primary function of the trade union, is not its main justification. Mr Enoch Powell and Professor Milton Friedman are no doubt right to assert that trade unions have done nothing to raise the living standards of the workers, though particular unions may have raised the standard of living of particular groups of workers through the use of monopoly power at the expense of other workers with less leverage on the labour market. That is not to say that trade unions have no value. They have psychological importance, especially in large-scale industry where the trade union is something to which the worker feels he belongs and which will nurture his interests whether they be wages, industrial safety, job security or justice. When the details are established by collective contract these interests are far more sure and certain to be protected than if they rest merely on the personal whim of the foreman or manager.

The urge to band together with one's fellow workers is no doubt deeply rooted in human nature. The trade union, however, is not the only form it takes; for there is the 'profession', a word which is admittedly rather demoted in common parlance, by some who talk, for example, of 'a junk dealer by profession'. Yet it is generally associated with a rather limited range of activities such as the law, medicine, insurance, accountancy, management and administration, the land and engineering. Is there any essential difference between professions and trade unions? No doubt they have more in common than members of the professions usually care to admit. The professions are even to be credited with inventing the legal immunity for which trade unions in Great Britain at least are currently so much criticised. It was the university professors in the late twelfth century who were first exempted from the jurisdiction of the common law as long as they remained on their academic premises. Moreover, as many of them were religious clerks they also enjoyed a clerical claim to immunity. At first glance the member of a profession appears to be merely a kind of craftsman with a white collar and snob status. The difference is that as far as the traditional liberal professions at least are concerned, the insistence on integrity and the maintenance of professional standards are their main raison d'être. The trade unions which, after all, are not mainly craft unions, are mostly concerned with pay. This distinction is not meant to idealise the professions unduly. American doctors, for instance, seem to be much more of a trade union than a profession by this criterion. Moreover, the effect of inflation has been to erode professional standards, and to emphasise pay claims instead. For instance, the American Nurses Association, in an official statement, stated: 'Collective bargaining is not to be confused with Labour unionism. Collective bargaining is used by many organisations other than labour unions.'[1] This is a distinction without a difference. Yet it will be a shame if the real points of difference are not maintained. It would not be to anyone's advantage if the barristers were to lose interest in upholding the rule of law and devoted themselves single-mindedly to maximising their fees. Or, to take a specific example, there have been few spectacles more unedifying than the notorious strike of the Belgian doctors when several patients died because of lack of medical attention. No doubt professions should be subject to surveillance so that they do not adopt restrictive practices contrary to the interests of the community, but it would be regrettable if the baby were ejected with the bath water. The service society will be a more wholesome one if it involves adoption by the trade unions of standards of professional behaviour rather than that professional standards should evaporate and the professions become trade unions in all but name. It is not only that the professions proper abide by their own ethical standard, which may often conflict with the gross materialism of our times. It is also a question of diversifying loyalties. For at a time when the state seems intent on making its claims on the citizen ever more extensive and exclusive, almost any form of voluntary association which sets independent and honourable standards of behaviour and focuses men's minds on goals which are not prescribed by leviathan must be welcome to anyone concerned with the perpetuation of humane and civilised values.

[1] Adolf Sturmthal, ed., *White Collar Trade Unions*, University of Illinois Press, 1966, p. 352.

5

Retailing resurgent

The word 'retail' derives from the Old French, *retaille* meaning 'a piece cut off'. By the early fourteenth century this word had already appeared in Anglo-French with its modern English meaning: the sale of commodities in small quantities. Plainly the shaping and sizing of goods to suit the consumer is a vital economic function. To the hungry carnivore the work of the butcher in dividing up the animal's carcass is no whit less important than that of the livestock farmer who reared the beast before it came to market. To the man about town the tailor is no less essential than the manufacturer of the cloth from which his suit is cut. The schoolboy eager to make the most of his pocket money is unlikely to discriminate between the value to himself of the services of the man with the ice cream van and those of the lollipop maker. To all who accept the axiom that the object of production is consumption, it is indeed puerile to distinguish between the values of the different stages in the chain of related activities by which the consumer's satisfactions are fulfilled. Yet, curiously enough, such a distinction has been commonly made by the intelligent as well as the ignorant, from very early times. When Napoleon derided the British as a nation of shopkeepers, he was expressing more than a Latin prejudice, he was reflecting a widespread traditional dislike of retailers, which can be traced back to the ancient world.

In this context the intellectuals seem generally to have done little more than state with greater refinement an unreflecting popular bias. Aristotle, as we have seen, viewed retailing with disfavour since it reached beyond the confines of the domestic economy and led only to 'unnatural' kinds of acquisition. Cicero, though tolerant of the wholesale trade on the snobbish grounds that it might lead to the possession of a country estate, poured scorn on the poor shopkeeper. 'Vulgar we must consider those who buy from wholesale merchants to retail immediately; for they would get no profits without a great deal of downright lying.'[1]

---

[1] Quoted in Dorothy Davis, *A History of Shopping*, Routledge, 1966, p. 17.

The same picture of the grasping shopkeeper appears in *Piers Plowman* in medieval times:

> Punish in the pillories and stools of repentance
> The brewers, the bakers, the butchers, the cooks,
> For these are the men that do the most mischief
> To the poor people that buy by the parcel.

The assaults have continued up to today. One of G. K. Chesterton's best known poems is a song against the wicked grocer, written from his usual Burgundian point of view. In rather bleaker vein Sir Stafford Cripps observed (19 October 1945): 'Pre-war we had nearly three million people in distribution producing nothing.' Less explicitly, and in the even bleaker jargon of the technical economist, Nicholas Kaldor condemned retailing as a sector in which 'the marginal social product is likely to be appreciably below the marginal private product'.

Naturally this can only be a cursory and impressionistic indication of the invidious standing of the shopkeeper through the ages and clearly selective quotation is not proof, though in the examples given it points to a powerful tradition of hostility to the shopkeeper which calls for some explanation. It seems to arise from a widespread disposition to seek a scapegoat, to personalise economic evils which are all too often impersonal in character. It is a natural tendency in economically unsophisticated societies for people to lay the responsibility, for inflation for instance, on identifiable individuals or social groups. For example, the Emperor Diocletian, whose own government had consistently debased the currency, in AD 301 issued a proclamation in which he roundly blamed the shopkeepers for the universal price rise and made it a capital crime to raise prices anywhere in the Roman Empire.

This early exercise in prices and incomes policy proved as futile then as since. The normal mechanics of inflation unfortunately give retailers windfall profits which the ignorant see as its cause, not its consequence, and make them natural targets for the anger of the moralist who automatically accuses them of profiteering. If this leads the authorities to fix prices and impose rationing it only encourages the kind of evasions which make them still more unpopular. George Orwell pointed out in 1945, that British antisemitism was then actually on the increase, despite Hitler, and he attributed

---

[1]Quoted in Alexander Gray, *The Development of Economic Doctrine*, Longmans, 1948, p. 34.

this to the fact that British Jews were extensively engaged in selling food, clothes, furniture and tobacco. These were the very commodities which in wartime were in chronically short supply, with consequent overcharging, black-marketeering and favouritism. Indeed a great deal of antisemitism throughout European history plainly owed much to the fact that the Jew was typically a retailer and therefore the obvious scapegoat in times of economic adversity.

Thus the relatively poor status of the shopkeeper appears to be a survival into modern times of attitudes more appropriate to a primitive stage of economic development. In the household economy which Aristotle so much approved, where for the most part men produced for themselves what they needed and any kind of exchange, let alone retailing, was the exception rather than the rule, the producer and the consumer were for most of the time one and the same. In this idyllically simple economic order there was no distribution problem to vex the moralist. Broadly, the Labour theory of value could not be gainsaid when production was necessarily for use, the producer's own use that is, and the worker toiled only to satisfy directly the wants of himself and his family. When man had eaten of the tree of economic knowledge and started to engage first in barter, then in trade, and finally had graduated to the use of money, the distribution theory of his innocence would no longer suffice. An object valued in the household on account of the work which had gone into it might appear worthless when exposed to the merciless appraisal of the marketplace. What is more understandable than that in this new situation the producer should regard the market value as unjust, especially when it was damaging to his self-esteem?

Again, to venture away from the household to the exchange economy, entailed a new order of risk. The hazards of the former, such as drought, flood and harvest failure, were considerable, but they had the advantage of familiarity. Moreover, natural disasters, if beyond man's power to control, were yet acceptable as part of the dispensation of providence. On the other hand in the marketplace both producers and consumers, for the most part, found themselves at the mercy of external forces, but forces nevertheless of human origin which therefore lacked the providential or natural sanction to make them tolerable. It needed no startling perception to discern that acceptance of the rule of the marketplace often meant risking subjection to another's market power, and the smaller the market the greater the potential abuse. Thus in medieval times, in Britain and elsewhere, the authorities were constantly supervising the prices of necessities like bread and beer at the relatively small-scale markets and fairs, and watching for any attempt to hoard or to corner the market, expecially in foodstuffs, where a high monopoly price could mean starvation for the poor.

In principle the way to escape from monopoly exploitation, or the perils of dependence on the vagaries of weather and crops, was to widen the market, thus increasing the number of suppliers and averaging the impact of nature's caprice. Yet this was limited in medieval times by the derisory reach of the arm of the law, and the inadequacies of Gothic transport. As long as the economy remained confined within exiguous local markets, controls and restrictions were inevitable. The same logic applies today if a national state, such as modern India for instance, goes in for a protectionist policy, it leads to restriction and state control in its domestic economy. Unfortunately controls are usually conservative in the bad sense of setting out to protect established interests, and hinder the innovator. Medieval regulations, in retrospect, seem deliberately designed to prevent the division of labour between making and selling. The medieval town was 'a collection of craftsmen rather than of shopkeepers'.[1] The prevailing doctrine was that the craftsman should sell his own products. The three great commercial sins of the Middle Ages were forestalling, engrossing and regrating, and they were constantly forbidden by the authorities. Many historians accept these at their face value as various forms of consumer exploitation. Yet from another point of view they may be seen as inseparable from the growth of specialisation. Forestalling was buying outside the market and regrating was reselling at a higher price. But that is precisely what retailing is about. Engrossing again was making a corner in a commodity and forcing up the price. Yet where does hoarding end and wholesaling begin? The medieval town's rulers were, in fact, objecting to the development of a market economy in which specialisation in sales functions plays an indispensable part.

Thus the growth of retailing appears to have been the significant factor which transformed the impoverished, localised and, to the extent that it survived periodic natural disasters, self-sufficient medieval economy into the fundamentally free market economy of the modern western world. The further back we retrace our steps, certainly in English history, the more indivisible the products available because the more inadequate the retailer. The rich bought wholesale at the fairs: a whole sheep, a whole cheese, a cask of wine or a bale

[1] Davis, *A History of Shopping*, p. 7.

of cloth. Even humble people bought what seem to us now very large quantities of goods at rare intervals. And they paid a heavy price in the monotony of diet which these conditions imposed. The advance of retailing consisted, by definition, of breaking the bulk of those commodities and selling a larger quantity of a more standard range of goods at more frequent intervals to a wider public. How then did the poor provide for their needs?

If we go back no further than the eighteenth century, it is still plain that the bright lights and bow windows of the fashionable shops of Georgian London were beyond their reach. The answer is that in the back streets there was an enormous number of small low-turnover shops, highly labour intensive and of very low productivity. The poor man's chandler supplied goods of all sorts by the farthing-worth and might take caps or aprons as pledges when cash was not available. Everywhere there were pawn shops and a corresponding trade in secondhand goods, especially clothing, for only the rich could afford bespoke tailoring, and that is all the tailoring there was until comparatively recent times. This large secondhand trade undoubtedly hindered the development of modern mass marketing methods, though it provided for the needs of the time. A great deal of the energies of English society before the industrial revolution went into buying and selling, the bulk of it in the street markets. Then there was a whole army of hawkers and pedlars of every kind, including, by the late eighteenth century, thousands of Scotch drapers, who sold clothing and household linen on tick to the workers. Their importance may be grasped from the fact that when it was proposed in 1780 to bring in a shops' tax and as a sop to the shopkeeper to prohibit pedlars, the textile manufacturers of Glasgow, Lancashire and Yorkshire made a violent and successful protest on the grounds that without the services of these itinerent salesmen they would have to close down their mills.

Yet both the pedlar and the street trader belong to the low volume retailing of a past age. The pedlar provided a valuable service to the widely spread consumers of a pre-urbanised society: he was the travelling Woolworths of late medieval Europe. Again, it is difficult to exaggerate the contribution of the Yankee pedlar to the opening up of America, but it is instructive that the more prosperous ones usually settled down and opened up as general merchants in a small town, or in a big city; the Strauss Brothers who built up, and eventually bought up Macy's of New York were immigrant Bavarian Jews, who started their business careers on the road. The street trader belongs essentially to the old rural economy in which towns were mainly important as providing periodic markets where the farmers, and secondarily the artisans, sold what they themselves had produced. Specialisation in retailing could only come when shop-keeping became a full time activity quite separate from farming or handicrafts. Division of labour was, as ever, the clue to economic progress.

However, the distinction was slower to work itself out than one might expect. In 1831 a British census of adult males grouped to-gether in a special category those engaged in 'retail trade and handi-crafts', a category which included (besides building and road trans-port and some sections of the wholesale trade) a number of occupa-tions which were classified with manufacturing in later censuses.[1] Even well into the present century the shopkeeper was a processor, performing many tasks which are now within the province of the manufacturer. The butcher bought on the hoof and did his own slaughtering and dressing. The grocer sliced bacon, ground pepper and blended tea. Haberdashers bought cotton and thread by the pound, disentangled it and folded it into hanks for sale across the counter. In modern times the craftsman-retailer remains mainly in the luxury trades: in high class tailoring in London's Savile Row or Brooks Brothers of New York, in bespoke shoemaking virtually anywhere, and in the jewellery trade. In Tiffany's, for instance, the firm's silversmiths set its own gems in the building, while dowagers who do not want their pearls out of their sight can have them re-strung in front of their eyes in private rooms.

The growth of efficiency in retailing was for long greatly hampered by the lack of commonly recognised standards which now we take for granted. For instance, weights and measures and even currencies were bewildering in their variety, especially in Europe, until the French revolutionary armies imposed the metric system, and the greater the variety of measures the greater the scope for fraud.

Another drawback until well into the nineteenth century in Eng-land, for instance, was a shortage of currency. This was one reason for the development of the truck system. The shortage of coin led to a considerable amount of business being done on credit. Naturally shopkeepers differentiated between customers according to their credit status, a far cry from the fixed prices of efficient modern retail-ing. Credit status counted all the more because an Act of James I had made shopkeepers' books inadmissible as evidence in courts of law as proofs of debts over a year old, the assumption being that

[1]Phyllis Deane, *The First Industrial Revolution*, Cambridge University Press, 1965, p. 257.

they were usually faked. To the rich no doubt the credit system was a convenience for which they paid in higher prices. To the poor, who bought haberdashery and household goods from tallymen and paid back by weekly instalment, tradesmen's debts often became a form of bondage with the constant awful threat of the debtor's prison in the background.

A situation favourable to modern mass retailing appeared in England in the second half of the nineteenth century. This was when a sufficiently large number of prosperous working-class customers concentrated in big urban centres to make large-scale organisation worth while. In earlier times this conditior had applied in only one trade and in only one place, namely to beer in London. For a disproportionate amount of the incomes of the London poor went on drink. Thus, as Dorothy Davis puts it,

> Beer, as sold in London, was the first consumer commodity to be mass produced under modern factory conditions and sold to the public for cash at fixed prices by 'pure' retailers. About one house in fifteen in London in the middle of the century was a public house of some sort, and they tended to be thickest on the ground in the poorer quarters.[1]

Since the middle of the last century in England, and only slightly later in other countries, there has been a progressive refinement of the retailing function with a gradual abandonment of quasimanufacturing, processing, or preparation of the articles for sale. With this increasing specialisation has come enhanced efficiency. Yet, strange to relate, the first to recognise the potentialities of the mass market were not sharpwitted businessmen but those utopian dreamers the Rochdale Pioneers. Perhaps it was their very idealism which enabled these originators of the cooperative movement to look at retailing in a new way and to make their most startling innovations. These were, in fact, neither the profit sharing principle of the dividend nor cash sales, but the branch system and the vertical integration of retailing and wholesaling which the possession of many branches made possible. The cooperative movement went on increasing its share of the total retail trade throughout Europe in the first half of the twentieth century and after the Second World War. In America it never made much headway, partly because its early development in New England was scotched by the outbreak of the civil war, but also because its appeal to proletarian solidarity evoked less response. One ingredient in its success in Europe was that it was

[1] *A History of Shopping*, p. 213.

a vehicle for the aspirations and a focus of the loyalties of the work-ing class, but, even in Europe, by the 1960s it was losing ground rapidly to the multiple stores. The latter had carried much further the idea of branch organisation and the corresponding economies in wholesaling arising from standard lines and bulk deliveries, while their managements were not hampered by democratically elected committees with old-fashioned ideas.

It seems astonishing, in retrospect, that the multiple stores did not come into their own much earlier. After all, the first cooperative stores appeared in 1844. Yet the multiples, though they made a spasmodic appearance in a few European countries, notably in the United Kingdom in the 1860s and 1870s, did not really get going until the end of the century. Then they spread rapidly in food, clothing, footwear and pharmaceuticals. This advance was halted by the First World War, but from 1925 onwards a new pace setter appeared, namely the variety chain store, following the pattern of the American five and ten cent store, and even, in the case of Wool-worth's, representing an extension of a vast, successful American organisation.

In the Anglo-Saxon countries, where the multiple store has made most headway, the independent retailer has fought back with the voluntary chain. This is an arrangement by which a group of inde-pendent retailers deal with a single wholesaler and, through dis-counts on minimum orders, members are able to share in the econ-omies of rationalised delivery of a standard range of items. They are then able to parallel the wholesaling economies of the big mul-tiple groups.

The department store, which is really a French invention, the Bon Marché – the world's first department store opened in Paris in 1872 – is a rather special example of the economies of large-scale buying based not on a large number of shops, but usually on the large shop or, more recently, a group of large shops selling a huge variety of merchandise – the Mitsukoshi store in Tokyo even furnishes brides and grooms and marriage ceremonies in the basement. Some indica-tion of the scale of operations is given by the example of Macy's, which with the ten other stores of its New York division for the first time rang up sales of three million dollars one Saturday during the 1965 Christmas season. Department stores are now a world pheno-menon, and even Moscow boasts its GUM facing the Kremlin across Red Square. These big stores set the pace for the retail trade in most of the world's great cities until 1914. After the 1914–18 war, however, the movement to the suburbs of the middle classes who were their main customers, plus the growth of the multiples which were more able to switch to suburban shopping centres, led generally to a weakening in the department store's position. In most countries it has been at most holding its market share since the Second World War. Some have responded to this movement of their customers by branching out into the mail order business.

The penultimate expression of the retailing ideal is to be found in the supermarket, where everything is prepackaged, where the salesman has disappeared and all that is left is the female cashier, the modern version of the Edwardian woman imprisoned in the draper's cage, who spent her days taking in the cash and transmitting the change in brass containers along a network of strategically placed wires. The interesting thing is that this concentration on the pure selling function, with all the preparatory work of grading, packaging, weighing, and measuring being done by the manufacturers in advance, has enabled the shops adopting the technique enormously to extend the range of their merchandise. So, increasingly, the traditional demarcations between different types of retailer have been eroded, the process being made all the more rapid by the withering of resale price maintenance. The ultimate to date is the automat, which even substitutes a coin-operated machine for the hapless lady cashier, and is literally push-button selling.

In one way we have come a full circle. For until recently the advance of retailing could be defined as the increasing tendency of the system to provide the consumer with the goods he wants in quantities small enough to suit his tastes at whatever time he requires them. However, in food, the widespread ownership of deep freeze equipment is leading to wholesale purchase by the consumer. Indeed an average citizen in modern America may buy in bulk like a European aristocrat in feudal times.

It is clear from the preceding survey that distribution always has absorbed a significant proportion of the energies of civilised peoples. At present, when between a third and a half of the final prices of industrial and consumer goods, in Britain for instance, are accounted for by the costs of distribution, it is a sector not to be ignored. Yet only a minority of economists has shown much interest in it. The dominant Galbraithian view is that distribution is of secondary importance, a puppet, even if a large puppet, of the economic order, performing according to the dictates and manipulations of the holders of industrial corporate power. In fact this seems to be at best an obsolete picture of the economy. It could be argued that, following the industrial revolution, the initiative in economic development came from the manufacturing sector practically until the end of the century. It is arguable, but more contestable, that with the durable goods revolution of this century distribution has had only a supporting role, with manufacturing taking the star part. However, it now appears that just as the merchant was the dominant entrepreneur in eighteenth-century England, so increasingly it is the supermarketeer who is more and more directly the advance guard of Western economies and who at the times when it is fashionable to deny the reality of consumer sovereignty and the efficacy of competition is in fact communicating the consumer's preference to the producer and imparting to the economy an intensity of competition, unknown since the heyday of Victorian laissez-faire.

This is more than a mere assertion. The supermarket has given a new edge to retailing competition because of its singleminded pursuit of profit, for the whole operation hinges around the computation of profit per linear foot. 'No item on the shelves of a super is in a haven. It must sell or be eliminated.'[1] This ruthless attention to market performance reflects back on manufacturing costs. The Great Atlantic and Pacific Tea Company, the food industry leader in the United States, strove for a 12 per cent gross profit once it adopted supermarket operation in the 1930s, though before that it was nearer 20 per cent. Such reduced margins have made skilful buying all the more important, thus putting the pressure on the manufacturer's costs, have also led the Atlantic and Pacific Tea Company towards backward integration into manufacture, thus directly subjugating the producers to market forces.

That the closest control over manufacturing is possible without any change of ownership has been classically demonstrated by that remarkable British concern Marks and Spencer. It lays down detailed specifications to which its suppliers must conform. There must be no blemishes on any bananas. It determines the breed of chicken required and specifies exactly how the birds are to be killed, plucked, stored and packed. Marks's shirts must be able to withstand up to fifty launderings. To maintain these standards the firm keeps its own quality inspectors overlooking production lines. For those firms which cannot both reach these standards and also make a good profit there are teams of M and S production engineers, works accountants, and food technologists ready to move in and teach them how to make money. So in this instance the suppliers actually lose their autonomy to the retailer: here without question

[1] Frank J. Charvat, *Supermarketing*, New York, Macmillan, 1961, p. 77.

market criteria are supreme.

The growing power of the retailer over the manufacturer in the postwar period has arisen because of the stiffer competition at the selling outlets being passed back along the line to the producer. This process was delayed in the immediate postwar phase by the system of resale price maintenance which had flowered during the depression years; r.p.m. was now a barrier to efficiency because it usually worked by obliging the manufacturer to apply sanctions against the innovator who wanted to cut prices and increase turnover, in order to protect the less competent. However, while governments contemplated the repeal of r.p.m. the more vigorous spirits of the retailing fraternity were already undermining it. Department stores and multiples circumvented the problem of the price-maintained branded article by marketing their own brands. Then, developing in America in the 'fifties, and arriving in Europe in the 'sixties, trading stamps effectively undercut the maintained prices and accustomed the public to the idea that the manufacturer's prescribed price was not sacrosanct and that discounts were not only desirable but feasible.

In Europe other restrictions were also being bypassed by the vigorous new generation of retailers. Restrictions on shop hours at their worst in Great Britain and Western Germany were, for instance, particularly surmounted by the development of mail order selling on the one hand and of automatic vending on the other. The latter has spread from its long-established use in confectionery, matches etc. initially to groceries and drinks and latterly to stockings, cleaning materials, toys, stationery and toiletries.

Meanwhile by about 1964 the resale price maintenance system had, almost everywhere, come under political attack and with the repeal in most countries of the legislation supporting it has since been in retreat all over the western world.

There still remain in Europe many restrictions inherited from the depression, even though they have been modified. The British retain their curious limitation on shop hours which ensures that shops are open when most people are working and shut in their leisure hours. The continentals are still lumbered with laws passed during the depression, to protect the small trader and which now hinder the growth of large scale retailing. Thus the French, with a smaller population than the British, have 50 per cent more shops – one might call them a nation of Poujadist shopkeepers. Continental restrictions curtail new entry, take the form of outdated hygiene and sanitary regulations affecting the grouping of goods and their conditions of sale including limits on times of bargain sales, and even include discriminatory taxation. It is because government in Great Britain before the war did not set out to protect the independent retailer against the big operators that British retailing is generally so superior to that on the Continent. Indeed for those who are looking for the silver lining in the generally overcast picture of the British economy it is provided by Marks and Spencer's and Tesco's, the dynamic supermarket chain. One of the curious effects of this relative efficiency in the retailing sector, which is the direct result of unhampered competition, has been to make many British people fearful of the prospect of increased competition in the Common Market. For the one thing which public opinion is seized of on this subject is the higher prices in mainland Europe's shops. In fact the comparative cheapness of the goods in British shops is more of a tribute to their superior selling organisation than an indictment of the Community's common agricultural policy. In point of fact the Common Market should provide an opportunity for the nation of shopkeepers to extend the operation of its merchandising skills and multiply its multiples throughout the length and breadth of the European continent.

6

Services and the quality of life

There is nothing so powerful, said Max Nicholson, as the idea whose time has come, and there is little doubt that 1970, European Conservation year, no less, was the time when the environment issue came into its own. In that year, in the Western world in general and in Britain in particular (where both Labour and Conservative governments in turn appointed a Minister for the Environment) suddenly the exhortations to expand or perish gave way to dire warnings that the very process of expansion was goading society towards disaster.

This change of fashion, as violent as anything Dior ever did, calls for some explanation. No doubt it owed something to a natural revulsion against the grossness and naivety of the growth doctrine. Partly it was the effect of some spectacular and well publicised pollution scandals. Fundamentally it was due to the waning of the Soviet economic threat which at the time of the launching of Sputnik One had appeared to be supremely dangerous.

Certainly there is no need to regret the passing of Western growth-mania; the danger is that one unbalanced state of mind may only be succeeded by another. In essence the new message is sensible enough; it is that the singleminded pursuit of industrial growth is depriving us of the free services of nature, such as clean air, water, soil and silence. Unfortunately it is also tailormade to fit the purposes of all improving liberals and exponents of the higher journalism, offering as it does boundless oportunities for denouncing society for its collective guilt. The range of potential catastrophe it presents is extensive, varied and intriguing. For a start there is the growth of world population, likely, according to UN forecasts, to double by the end of the century This threatens to cause, either singly or in combination, famine, raw material scarcity, disease, and war. Meanwhile the rising consumption of fuel is creating so much carbon dioxide that it threatens to upset the balance of the biosphere, leading to a rise of air temperature which in turn will melt the ice caps and bring a new flood. Alternatively, jet aircraft trails may surround the world with clouds, which will keep out the sun's rays and bring a new ice age, though by that time the air may be so dirty that in any case we shall all have choked to death. In the interin, not only the lakes, but even the world's seas will have been poisoned by chemicals which will kill all the fish. Even if the human race survives these horrors, it is likely to receive its quietus along with all other wild and domestic vertebrates, by the build up of DDT and other pesticides, herbicides and fungicides in its tissues.

Even if fractionally true, such dangers hardly invite complacency. Yet most of them are unnecessarily apocalyptic. For example, the U.N. forecast of world population – a subject incidentally, in which professional soothsayers ever since Malthus have shown an astounding proclivity to err – is in essence a simple projection at the present rate of increase of 2 per cent a year. According to Kahn and Weiner the forecast 6.9 to 7 billion people is likely to be wrong 'by a billion or two' because it overlooks the fact that by 1980 birth control techniques are likely to be simple and cheap and should thereafter have a substantial effect on the birth rates in the underdeveloped world. Again, the recent advance in producing higher yielding grain should alone postpone world starvation. Next consider the belief that the world will run out of fuel and raw materials. It looks superficially plausible. Yet we recall that only in 1956 when all the Western nations were dreading an oil shortage, they were actually poised on the eve of a glut. Besides, exhaustive studies by Resources for the Future have shown that there are no foreseeable limits to supplies of basic natural resources. Even if there were technology is constantly producing new substitutes for conventional materials and lowering the costs of alternative sources of energy.[1] Moreover, even if we assume an increasing final demand for goods, expected developments in material science promise increased durability, strength, and reusability, for instance of steel and fibres thus requiring a smaller volume of these materials for the same final output. Again, the rest of the world does not have to follow the pattern of material civilisation which has established itself in North America. For instance, if electronic communication systems develop at their present hectic rate many people will be able to work at home and the provision of transport systems to cater for rush hour volumes of traffic will be unnecessary. The odds are that the United States pattern of car ownership will not establish itself universally; instead, more eco-

[1] Neil Jacoby and F.G. Pennance, *The Polluters, Industry or Government?*, Institute of Economic Affairs, 1972.

nomical hiring systems should become typical, especially in crowded countries. Nor surely is the wasteful, noisy pollution-prone internal combusion engine fated to remain for much longer the dominant source of overland propulsion. Such dismal assumptions, which are still the staples of economic forecasting, are based on what is already an old-fashioned view of the economy as primarily a collection of goods. In fact the striking characteristic of the new service society is, as we have said, an increasing consumption of services, which often displace goods. For example, a TV Console connected to a data bank will be much more than a substitute for thousands of books, and should eventually displace newspapers, too.

In any event, the increasingly dominant feature of the service economy is the reduction in hours of work, and obviously a leisured society is bound to place more value on the charms of an unpolluted environment than one in which workers spend most of their waking hours in dark satanic mills. Conservationists should take heart from the fact that while the number of despoilers of the countryside is growing, the number of people determined to enjoy the country-side is growing too. One thing which apparently helped to persuade the British Labour leadership that dramatic declarations of anti-pollutive intent would be electorally beneficial was the realisation that the five million anglers in Britain actually outnumbered the spectators at soccer matches.

However, there was another element in the conventional pro-nouncements of the ecology lobby which appealed to Socialists even more. This was that most of its acolytes tend to blame the sins of pollution on the immorality of the social order. This attitude springs partly from the romantic, back-to-nature, back-to-the-Middle Ages, anti-industrial, anti-urban yearnings of some literary folk who, like William Morris a century ago, are still dreaming of an England small and white and clean. It is also a stick with which to beat the capitalist, who is identified as the archpolluter (literally the filthy capitalist) who goes by the adage 'where there's muck there's money' and doesn't care how dirty he makes the world provided he makes a profit.

Sometimes these criticisms are extremely perverse. For instance, John Barr in an otherwise admirable survey, *Derelict Britain* (Penguin Books, 1969), criticises the brick companies for making huge holes in the ground while extracting clay and goes on to express indignation at the fact that these companies make a profit by charging local authorities for dumping their rubbish, and the Electricity Generating Board for depositing its power station ash.

Worse still, after the holes are filled, the brick companies sell the regained areas for development. Barr draws the peculiar conclusion that the local ratepayers and the nation's electricity consumers are subidising the brick industry. Such fantasy erupts no doubt from his impatience at the fact that many owners of holes near urban areas refuse to entertain any reclamation schemes 'because a derelict dry pit is more valuable than just about anything that might replace it'. Yet, except to the perfectionist who wants wrongs remedied immediately, this particular example seems strangely providential in that so many interests stand to gain in a process of voluntary co-operation which purges the original environmental sin. No doubt it is with some a desire to put things right in a hurry (as presumably in Mr Barr's case) just as with others it is an authoritarian state of mind, which leads to the advocacy of strong, though often arbitrary, governmental measures. The amusing thing is that this panacea for pulchritude – centralised planning – is identical with the former nostrum for growth, and is advocated by the same people. Social aims may change, but the bureaucratic mind is always with us.

A good example of this simpleminded faith in the healing powers of government agencies occurs in a pamphlet produced by the British Labour Research Department for the Annual Conference of Labour Women on *Pollution and the Environment* (1970). This proposes a comprehensive family planning service to prevent over population; a central executive agency to deal with sewage disposal, water supply and river pollution; a sea pollution authority; a national executive agency to coordinate and take initiatives in refuse disposal; a land reclamation agency to restore derelict areas; an inspectorate to encourage noise abatement in industry; and finally an integrated government department to treat environmental problems as unities.

Unfortunately for this approach the record of government bodies is at least as bad as that of private profit-seeking concerns. The Soviet Union provides the most hair-raising examples. The lower reaches of the Volga were turned into a series of lakes intended by Stalin's engineers to provide hydroelectric power, to irrigate thousands of square miles of semidesert and to change the climate of the whole region. In practice it salinated huge areas of croplands and the lakes have been filled with rotting vegetation, the smell of which is so awful that even airplane pilots avoid flying over them.[1]

---

[1] Andrei D. Sakharov, *Progress Coexistence and Intellectual Freedom*, Penguin Books (Pelican), 1969, p. 96.

In some ways still worse, despite the appalling example of Lake Erie, from which they might surely have learnt, the Russians have polluted the enormous Lake Baikal and overfishing has practically destroyed the sturgeon (and therefore the caviar) of the Volga and the Caspian.

It is worth noting too that in western countries some of the worst pollution is the fault of government agencies or nationalised industries. The notorious DDT spraying of the Dutch elm trees in American suburbs which caused the death of so many American robins that it inspired the title of Rachel Carson's *Silent Spring* was the work of American municipal authorities. In Britain again civil servants only just failed to place London's third airport in Stansted, which would have desecrated one of the most charming and historic parts of rural Essex. However, the National Coal Board has succeeded where Whitehall failed. It has achieved historic success in dirtying the nation's air by producing too little smokeless fuel for the needs of the inhabitants of smokeless zones.

This shows that the mere assumption or possession of powers to regulate the quality of the human environment, even though it is sometimes a necessary means, is not in itself sufficient to achieve that end. Power is practically useless without some consistent criterion for its use. What appears at first sight as a simple matter of prohibition usually becomes a complex matter of regulation. Some acts of power often end by achieving the opposite effect to that which was intended. For example, town planning in Britain has the laudable aims of maintaining a green belt around towns and preserving beautiful and historic buildings inside them. In practice one result of the green belts being zealously preserved for a limited range of uses, some of which do not pay, because of the nearness of the town (farming for instance may be hindered by vandals or dogs) is that the land becomes derelict. At the same time the refusal of town planners to let the town expand into the green belt raises the price of land inside the town and makes the demolition of beautiful historic buildings more profitable.

Moreover, in the case of town planning, what appear at first sight to be a body of consistent criteria are often no more than the reflection of the subjective preferences of a particular planning school. Thus the prewar British ribbon development of houses built adjacent to the main highway (a practice made generally feasible by the motor car) was much condemned. There is now a perfectly reputable school of thought which regards this form of development as an ideal called the 'linear city'. Nor is the green belt concept any longer sacrosanct, even in Britain. Not long ago a government regional plan *Strategy for the South East,* proposed growth corridors based on main transportation lines between London and new satellite cities.

At first sight the problem of air pollution might appear more susceptible to regulation. Plainly it is possible to require factories to limit the volume of dirty smoke which their chimneys emit. Yet what degree of purity should the authorities stipulate? The question is important, for, generally, the greater the degree of purity required the more than proportionately higher the cost of achieving it. Certainly a government can impose aesthetic standards or purity technical standards of health or safety or whatever, regardless of cost, but these are hardly the assumptions one can make in a democracy which must by its nature require the decisions of authority to reflect some calculus of the balance of individual interests, rights, and obligations.

One of the most popular techniques of making such calculations in recent years has been cost-benefit analysis. This attempts to quantify the neighbourhood effects for good or ill of such things as transport projects, and claims to have the advantage of going beyond the immediate profit and loss criterion of the businessman. This figuring is usually done from a welfare point of view. In that context it is open to the criticism that it gives a spurious impression of precision to what are predominantly shadow prices which themselves mirror little more than highly subjective preferences on the part of the analysts. Yet surely where such issues as the beauties of the environment are at stake, the subjective element must be even more pronounced than in the case of a welfare calculus?

A more hopeful approach is to try to make the market situation a true projection of the total balance of advantages. If within the existing institutional arrangements the claims of beauty and amenity are underrepresented, then we need to change our institutional arrangements so that, in the quest of profit, the external diseconomies will be minimised. How then do we make the invisible hand more responsive to amenity needs? Happily the revival of free enterprise economic thinking in the last decade has generated many novel ideas which, not long ago academic, are, because of the advance of electronic gadgetry, now assuming practical shape. For instance, it is not only feasible but before long should not even be expensive, to establish a system of taxing traffic congestion, by installing meters on vehicles which are activated in high congestion areas. This will tend to ration space to those who are most prepared to pay for it and at the same time should provide finance for road works to help mitigate congestion in the future.

We must remember that what economists blithely call the free services of nature are often only decently maintained at a cost. The idea, to which the British unfortunately hold rather firmly, at least when they are in their own country, is that the seashore should be free. This tempts seaside local authorities which must keep their beaches clean to let them out for various industrial and commercial purposes, including power stations, quarries and sewage works, and thus continually reduce the amount of 'free' beach available for holiday makers. If they are to be preserved neither beaches nor beauty spots in the country should be free of charge. The conservationists' best hope of success is to apply as far as possible the rule that he who benefits shall pay.

It is mainly the rigidity of the bureaucratic mind which prevents the authorities in Western countries from making more use of market pricing to facilitiate the work of the town planner. Ideally there should be a tax on ugliness equivalent, say, to a standard architect's fee on the more atrocious buildings. Regrettably, as beauty is so much a quality in the eye of the beholder, and as the lack of generally accepted architectural standards is so obvious, such a tax would be certainly capricious, probably vindictive, and presumptively punitive towards innovatory styles. More pertinent in resolving the conflicts of territorial interests and visual prejudices is the ingenious suggestion of F. G. Pennance[1] that development rights, i.e. planning permissions, should be put up for sale. Thus the opponents of a development could band together in order to purchase the development rights of what they regarded as an eyesore, an inconvenience or a threat to the dignity of the neighbourhood. Disputes over land use could still be determined at a public hearing – but the only voices would be those of the bidders and the auctioneer.

If those who, either as producers of consumers, impose costs on their neighbours, are to be correspondingly charged or taxed for their iniquities, what about those – like the beekeeper who helps adjacent gardens grow – whose activities put their neighbours morally in their debt? Generally there is no call to do anything except relax and enjoy the external economies which a kindly fate has bestowed. However, though it is hard to be precise, there are some cases where neighbourhood effects are substantial enough to justify the payment of bounties to those who create them. Operas, ballets

[1] *Housing, Town Planning and the Land Commission*, Hobart Papers no. 40, IEA, 1967, p. 17.

and symphony orchestras are nearly everywhere unprofitable but, especially where they achieve a high artistic standard, enhance the glamour of the cities or the countries which sustain them. The British Royal Family, the Chelsea pensioners, and the Beefeaters are surely worth their keep if only because of the traditional pageantry which they add to the London scene. They make the capital a more exciting place to live in, thus intangibly adding to the Londoner's standard of living as well as providing an attraction to tourists and thereby adding more palpably to Britain's invisible earnings.

It should be possible further to add to the quality of life on this crowded planet by the offer of prizes to inventors of products, processes, or techniques which reduce the social cost of the economic activities to which they apply. Thus it might be possible to stimulate the development of more silent aircraft and automobile engines, or plastic packaging which decays a little time after disposal, or to make oil wastes from ships soluble and harmless to marine life.

The most far reaching suggestion comes from Dr Mishan whose book *The Costs of Economic Growth*[1] is a veritable jeremiad against the now fading growth mania in Western countries. He argues that the only escape from the hell on earth created by the thoughtless greed of industrial man is to make amenity rights, rights, that is, to clean air, water, privacy and unspoilt countryside, part of the freehold of each citizen. This proposal for legal reform contrasts happily with the flotilla of controlling agencies favoured by many who see the remedy for pollution as, essentially, the creation of punitive deterrents for deployment against the wicked capitalists. It is refreshing that, instead of adding to the discretionary powers of government, Mishan's proposals would in effect extent the range of common law rights. Though in some instances statute should provide guiding lines in defining, for example, the number of decibels tolerable at what ranges where the right to silence is violated, there should be ample scope for the courts to spell out detailed applications of the citizen's ecological entitlement. The aim should be to give everyone the opportunity for legal redress against annoyance from noisy aircraft, vehicles, motor mowers and other mechanical gadgets, as well as the growing plague of transistors. Every individual should also be able to enjoy his privacy and be protected against electronic bugging devices. Thus the ecological crisis, instead of affording an excuse for multiplying central constraints, should

[1] E.J. Mishan, *The Costs of Economic Growth*, Staples Press, 1967, Penguin Books, 1969.

provide the occasion for an environmental bill of rights.

The growth of leisure will make the protection of these environmental rights more urgent. By the end of the century something like a thirty-hour week should be general throughout the Western world. Holidays described by one writer as a 'major national obsession' of the French people will no doubt be unhinging all the other advanced nations, too, in the course of a generation. More disturbing, the great question of what to do with their time will no longer be merely the cause of delicious anguish among the affluent, but the source of a more tedious malaise among the many. Since the beginning of time, the energies of mankind have been largely absorbed in keeping the wolf, at first literally and then metaphorically, from the door. In perhaps half a century the world may be populated with characters from Chekhov, or there may be a mass acting out of the saga of the Beatles' undirected quest for Life's inner meaning. Yet the odds are strong that the shape of things to come is more like a global amusement park than a giant cherry orchard. Certainly the economy of the future will be rated more by its fun content than by its index of industrial production. Already the Danes have shown that, as a holiday centre, a forest yields several times its revenue from timber. Nor have the investment analysts been slow to recommend entertainment as a lively growth prospect. Thus there is no question of the capacity of capitalism to supply circuses in the future with the same alacrity as bread in the past.

Yet this is to reckon without the influence of politicians who have been busy discovering the problem of leisure. Up to a point their discovery is genuine, as there will surely be discontents among an increasingly idle population for which the market cannot cater not only because money of itself cannot buy contentment but because there is imperfect knowledge among the public even of the purchaseable possibilities of life. There is a perfectly reputable paternalist case for the state to support excellence in a variety of fields where it would not be commercially profitable. Lord Reith's view of the task of the BBC as the raising of the moral intellectual and aesthetic standards of the people is really the only justification for a state broadcasting service. Yet such paternalism becomes nauseating when it demands not merely a state service but a state monopoly. Lord Reith himself was not above jamming Radio Luxembourg when it started to steal his audience. The difficulty with the paternalist argument is that it can be used to justify anything.

For instance, why should not the state run its own newspaper as an example of high journalistic standards? The mind boggles at the range of possible applications of the principle of unqualified paternalism. Some limitation is necessary. The most useful and least dangerous role for the authorities is the salvage of cultural cinderellas such as classical music and some of the dramatic and visual arts. Even here tax concessions to induce individuals to sustain them are politically and aesthetically preferable because such a system diffuses decisions as to what shall receive support widely among the population instead of concentrating them among a few fallible men in pinstriped trousers. Even tax concessions are only an imperfect interim solution, until it is feasible to reduce direct taxation to the point where enough individuals feel disposed to support culture out of their disposable incomes. In other parts of the leisure field the less officialdom the better. There is a dreariness peculiar to Britain which the young especially resent and which can in large measure be traced to the inadequate state of sporting and other amenities, for the provision of which the town hall has come to be mainly responsible. Strangely enough, it is in the leisure sector that the early Fabian crusade for municipalisation or 'gas and water socialism' had its most enduring triumph. From the point of view of improving British morale there is no more urgent candidate for return to private ownership, no area more in need, through the market, of improving its responsiveness to the popular demand for an enhanced quality of life than the service of leisure.

7

The public service

This has been called the century of the common man, though judging by results to date even the commonest of men is unlikely to treat the epithet as complimentary. It would be more apt to say that it is the century in which the common man is what Americans call the 'fall guy' for everything his government does. In this perverse sense the whole world in now democratic; even the worst sorts of rulers now pretend to act in the name of the sovereign people, and it was perhaps predictable that the most oppressive of contemporary regimes should style themselves 'peoples' democracies'. Indeed it is a sound maxim that the more vociferously national leaders claim to be acting on behalf of their subjects, the more assiduous they are in maltreating them. The sad truth is that much of the claptrap about democracy is in the nature of an apologia or a cover up for what really has grown, namely the activities of government itself. And closely associated, indeed organically dependent on it, is the rise of the public bureaucracy. For truly this present epoch is not so much the century of the common man as the age of the official.

The bureaucratic phenomenon is now worldwide. It goes without saying that bureaucracy is the most salient characteristic of the Soviet political system. Long before taking power Lenin had said that bureaucracy was the 'organisational principle of revolutionary social democracy' and practice has not fallen short of the dictum. With the abolition of private ownership of property, economic power has passed into the control of the ruling clique and been assigned in detail to the apparatchiks: ever since, save during the brief interlude of the 'New Economic Policy' in the 1920s, economic priorities have been determined not by market forces but by administrative fiat. So much is common knowledge, less widely realised is how far bureaucratisation has also gone in the West. Admittedly the degree of surprise is not extreme in the case of, say, France, where the *étatiste* tradition remains strong. More disquieting is the way that the British and the Americans, whose common political tradition is so hostile to concentrated executive power, have in recent times succumbed to the centralisers even more readily than the continentals. For example, the British non-industrial civil service has grown from 116,000 in 1901 to 497,300 in 1970. The former figure, moreover, includes postal workers and the latter does not; we should add at least a further 300,000 to the latest tally to make the comparison just. In the United States over the same period Federal Government employment of all kinds has leapt from 239,000 to just short of three million. In both countries the increase far outstrips population growth. Nor is that all, for in both there has been a parallel rise in state, county, city and municipal employment comparable with that in the central administration. As a result, to take the American example, total employment in federal, state, and local government bodies now accounts for about one in seven of the working population whereas in 1950 it accounted for only one in ten.

These figures illustrate what looks like a ubiquitous trend, and despite the snags which as usual attend international statistical comparisons, the overall direction seems to be clear: it is towards the socialisation of mankind.

It is always a temptation to regard such tides of social change as irresistible and therefore futile to oppose. Certainly there has been no lack of social theorists more than ready to yield to such temptation. Schumpeter believed that bureaucratic socialism was the natural successor to corporate capitalism.[1] Capitalist hostility to bureaucracy he regarded as irrational and only to be explained by an unfortunate historical association of ideas. For the bourgeoisie only achieved power after destroying the irksome restrictions imposed on their trading and manufacturing activities by a monarchist bureaucracy. Yet Schumpeter thought that a corps of skilled bureaucrats was essential to make democracy a success since their professional efficiency would outweigh the amateur bumbling of elected rulers. This argument is, indeed, the commonsense justification for having a bureaucracy at all, but it does not explain why it should continue to grow, unless we are constantly electing over worse bumblers.

Among popular economic writers J. K. Galbraith has done most to develop Schumpeter's theory that big business fosters the growth of bureaucratic government. As he sums up in the last chapter of *The New Industrial State:* 'Increasingly it will be recognised that the mature corporation, as it develops, becomes part of the large administrative complex associated with the state. In time the line

[1] *Capitalism, Socialism and Democracy*, p. 206.

between the two will disappear.' How does this happen? Galbraith leans heavily on examples in the defence field. There, especially where the government is the main purchaser, and where long term research and development programmes are the rule, the supervisory activities and therefore the numbers of government servants must increase. More generally, he argues that the mature industrial corporation requires stability for its forward planning and therefore welcomes Keynesian policies, designed to secure full employment, and the larger the public sector the easier such policies are to apply. He even interprets the growth of state intervention in education as primarily an attempt to ensure that big business obtains the trained manpower it needs.

One weakness of this analysis of Galbraith's is that, though it claims to diagnose a worldwide trend, it merely highlights some aspects of American experience in the period since the Second World War. Yet even in the American case he fails to show that the influence of the big industrial corporations is decisive. His examples from the defence field prove nothing. High defence spending doubtless inflates the number of bureaucrats supervising companies employed on defence contracts. But this will happen whether the firms concerned are big or small, though as a matter of fact the bigger and therefore the fewer the companies involved, the fewer civil servants should be needed for dealing with them. In defence production, therefore, the big corporation should lead to the employment of fewer bureaucrats not more. Again, the pursuit of Keynesian policies, though in itself usually conducive to collectivism, should not be any more collectivist in an economy which was the stamping ground of large industrial corporations than a Marshallian utopia where a myriad firms were engaged in perfect competition. For the chief Keynesian innovation was the unbalanced budget, designed to jack up aggregate demand to the point of full employment. Admittedly the Keynesian specification could be satisfied in an anticollectivist way by holding expenditure steady while cutting taxes, but governments are usually reluctant to sacrifice revenue when they have the agreeable alternative of sanctioning a bevy of pet departmental spending schemes. As for the idea that government is intervening increasingly in education in order to make life easy for the personnel departments of the corporate giants, this has more than a touch of the fanciful, and no doubt derives from the fallacy of misplaced concreteness, in that he treats the 'industrial system' (Galbraith's own collective title for the rag bag of large corporations) as a unitary personality with its own urges, desires and ambitions.

The expansion of Government in the United States has thus owed little to the growth of corporate power: how much less then can it be the cause of the parallel, but often greater, expansion of government in other parts of the world where the industrial corporation is far less developed!

We owe the most useful work on the subject to date to those less publicised economists who have analysed the rise of public expenditures: for broadly the size of the Civil Service corresponds to the scale of government spending. Frederick Pryor has shown that in highly developed countries public consumption expenditures swallow a much larger proportion of the national income than in the countries of the underdeveloped world.[1] Moreover, empirical evidence strongly supports the theory that economies changing from the rural agricultural to the urban industrial type considerably increase their public sectors' share of total spending. The one major exception to this trend curiously enough was Great Britain, where during the whole of the 19th century the ratio of public expenditures to national income showed no upward trend. Pryor further demonstrates that, since 1913, most countries, which have had rising national incomes per head, and rising populations, have displayed a tendency for their public expenditures to become evermore centralised – that is, central government spending has gradually been overtaking, and often taking over, that by local authorities.

In the same post-1913 period the growth of *total* public expenditures has nevertheless been very uneven and this demands an explanation which is more than an account of those forces which steadily push most societies towards higher public spending.[2] Messrs Peacock and Wiseman provide just such an explanation in the peoples' taxable capacity, though what they mean by this phrase is less the taxpayer's ability than his willingness to pay. Normally this is stable but it can shift if there is a serious crisis, for example, the two world wars or, in the American case at least, the great slump. This creates a 'displacement effect' displacing, that is, the tax ceiling which the citizen will tolerate. When the crisis is over, the ceiling tends to remain where it is rather than descend to its earlier level, and this allows the government to reduce one form of public expenditure, such as defence, while typically substituting some other

[1] F.L. Pryor, *Public Expenditures in Communist and Capitalist Nations*, Allen & Unwin, 1968, p. 52.
[2] A.T. Peacock and J. Wiseman, *The Growth of Public Expenditure in the United Kingdom*, Oxford University Press, 1962.

form of spending, such as welfare.

This ratchet effect, this tendency of high public spending levels to survive after wars, owes much to politicians eager to maintain expenditures which enhance their own prestige. It also owes a little to war's brutal way of exposing blemishes in the social fabric. The Battle of Waterloo led to the appointment of Lord Brougham's Committee to examine popular education. The Boer War's medical reports on recruits focused attention on the workers' poor physique. War puts millions of breadwinners into uniform and obliges governments to assume responsibilities for their dependents, thus creating social benefits which, after demobilisation, it is awkward to relinquish. The rhetoric, the propaganda and the uncritical atmosphere of wartime breed extravagant popular hopes which politicians seeking popularity eagerly promise to fulfil. The citizens of a democracy engaged in a ruinous war invariably expect, like the children of Israel in the desert but with less justification, to dwell, when hostilities are over, in a land flowing with milk and honey. For example, in Great Britain in the course of the First World War, at a time when housebuilding had ceased for the duration, came the political undertaking to provide homes fit for heroes to live in. Thus began the municipalisation of England – and even more of Scotland – that process whereby local authorities now own 30 per cent of the nation's homes. During the Second World War, when the British economy was virtually bankrupt, the Beveridge plan appeared, with its guarantee of social security to all. So began the welfare programme which now absorbs a quarter of the British national income.

Crises, then, nourish collectivism, they do not usually dismantle it, unless, as when the Roman Empire collapsed, they concurrently dismember society and demolish civilisation. Ordinarily, the scaling down of government calls for time, patience and the absence of catastrophe. Happily there is some reason to hope that these conditions are now widely applicable, that the phase of fast growing public expenditures may at last be not only coming to an end, but even going into reverse. Public consumption in the European Community for instance has stuck around the 14 per cent mark for the last decade. Admittedly during the same period, in the United States and Great Britain, it continued to rise, but this was perhaps the result in each instance of temporary aberration (or perhaps a crisis in the peacock and Wiseman sense) to wit the Vietnam war in the one case and the Wilson Government in other. More significantly Frederic Pryor in *Public Expenditures in Capitalist and Communist Nations* found that during the period 1950 to 1962 the share of the national incomes taken by public consumption actually fell in groups of both capitalist and communist countries. Moreover, the degree of centralisation of expenditures fell too. So it seems that the slide towards collectivism is losing momentum. Why? In Pryor's view because the richer the community the smaller the proportion of its output represented by the necessities of life. And as the 'necessities' are easiest, the 'luxuries' hardest, to allocate administratively, the area of economic life where public administration best applies must contract. Moreover, argues Pryor, as market economies grow, income inequalities within them diminish. So, for a given rise in public expenditure's share of the national income, the more advanced the economy, the more numerous the taxpayers required to finance it, the more widespread the resentment aroused, and the stonger the opposition provoked.

Statistics thus imply that the modern bureaucratic era may now be drawing to a close and that the public sector everywhere, even in the countries of the Eastern bloc, may at last be poised for retreat. How should we interpret this development? It is possible that industrialisation and urbanisation, and the more complicated society they bring with them, do involve an increase in state activity which, though inescapable, is also once for all. The new post-industrial, service-dominated society may, in its turn, witness a gradual reversal of public sector growth, mainly because, in an age of rising expectations, the mass of the people, whether in Posnan or Paris, find increasingly that it is the public domain which bars the way to the fulfilment of their personal economic goals.

Such, then, may be the shape of things to come. But the notion, however appealing to the tidy mind, that the amount of bureaucracy is, even approximately, a function of the stage of economic development, looks dubious when seen against the backcloth of history. The ancient world exhibited, in countries at much the same economic levels the extremes of zero bureaucracy and bureaucracy run riot. On the one hand many Greek city states were ruled entirely by amateurs chosen by lot, while on the other, the empires of Egypt, Assyria, Persia, of the Alexandrian Greeks, of Rome and Byzantium, early displayed in its most extravagant form the workings of Parkinson's law. In Europe in more recent times widely varying degrees of bureaucracy have been found contemporaneously in different, but economically comparable, countries. For instance, Bagehot tells us that at the expulsion of Louis Philippe the civil functionaries in France were said to amount to 807,030 individuals, and that this civil army was more than double the military. Yet at this time the British civil service totalled only about 16,000. Until the Northcote – Trevelyan reforms, indeed, intelligent amateurs administered the British state. Until then there were only two bureaucratic models in Europe: the French and the Prussian. Both grew up as the instruments of absolute monarchy, serving respectively the goals of Louis XIV and Frederick the Great. Both were at least partly the product of geography, for both countries were so placed on the mainland of Europe that they had long land frontiers to defend. Thus, as in the Roman Empire, administrative absolutism developed side by side with military autocracy. They evolved together if only because, as an army expands, so also must the tax revenues which support it, and as these grow more burdensome the collectors multiply still faster, for tax gathering is notoriously subject to the law of diminishing returns.

Until recently Great Britain avoided both militarism and bureaucracy. Before the present century the last large British standing army was Cromwell's, and the British people never forget how Cromwell used it for parliament's otherthrow. For two and a half centuries geography allowed the British to indulge their preference for personal liberty over military might because, surrounded as they were by sea, a good navy was all they needed to make them secure.

A wider view of history thus gives short shrift to the notion that bureaucracies must thrive as economies advance. Rather the active influences have been the necessities of war or the threat of war, the prevailing public philosophy, especially in relation to welfare, and the weight of the tax burden which the people will accept. The so-called technological imperatives which are supposed to make for monster government invariably on closer examination prove to be still further aspects of war and welfare. If the war danger recedes and (in Britain at least) if welfare's shotgun marriage with the state can be dissolved, there is every chance of eroding the public domain and diminishing the number of retainers who live off it. Yet the question still arises whether this is desirable. Given the choice should we, as Professor Galbraith has argued, welcome the advances of *homo bureaucraticus,* or should his blandishments be scorned as a sterner, older and decidedly Anglo-Saxon political tradition intimates? The time is ripe for such a rebuttal. Both Nixon's low profile and Heath's new style are explicit reactions against the government of their predecessors which was both excessive and excessively verbal. But are these reactions merely reactionary or are they valid for the long term?

An argument which must weigh with both leaders is the sheer

inefficiency of bureaucracy. As Bagehot said: 'It is an inevitable defect that bureaucracy will care more for routine than results; or as Burke put it "That they will think the substance of business not to be much more important than the forms of it".' Again, if allowed to, the bureaucrats would regulate everything in sight, multiplying their own numbers at great expense to the public purse. Bagehot also observed that a skilled bureaucracy 'is, though it boasts of an appearance of science, quite inconsistent with the true principles of the art of business'. This art he believed resulted from combining specialists with non-specialists, the former to scrutinise the trees and the latter to keep an eye on the wood. Bureaucrats always take the worm's eye view and lack perspective.[1] This all sounds very general criticism, but it is just as true now as in Bagehot's day. The economic performance of the Communist economies which are run by officials at all levels according to rules and directives is patently inferior to that of the West's market economies working for profit, and in the West itself the phrase 'public enterprise' is almost always a contradiction in terms. Communist managers have in recent years achieved the incredible results of Russia importing grain, and Cuba importing sugar. In Britain the performance of nationalised industries has been outstandingly secondrate and it is the constant endeavour of the authorities to impose conditions which shall force them to simulate the behaviour of competitive private enterprise or to install managers who behave like competitive private entrepreneurs.

Yet bureaucracy's inefficiency matters less than its menace to personal freedom; for the more extensive its operations the more denial there is of 'the habit of spontaneous action for a collective interest' as J.S. Mill put it (in his *Principles of Political Economy*) and the more the people are deprived of the freedom to develop their faculties. At the end of his essay on Liberty Mill put the point still more eloquently: 'A state which dwarfs its men in order that they may be more docile instruments in its hands even for beneficial purposes – will find that with small men no great thing can really be done.'

This century has not lacked examples to illustrate Mill's text. Modern Russia is a bureaucracy *par excellence*, corresponding exactly to the scornful definition which Lenin had once propounded before he came to power – 'privileged persons divorced from the people and standing above the people'. Yet, despite his assurance that that was not the way the 'armed proletariat' would behave once

[1] Walter Bagehot, *The English Constitution* (1867), Fontana, 1963, p. 194.

in control, his words exactly distill the personality of what has emerged as the Soviet elite. Milovan Djilas indeed describes the bureaucrats as a 'new class', the leading characteristic of which is that it uses, enjoys, and disposes of nationalised property as if that property were its own. To secure this enviable degree of power and privilege the new class busies itself with repression of all criticism which might undermine those privileges. Djilas's new elite is not peculiar to European Communist states. The most recent example is in Cuba where the top Party officials are known as 'Alfistas' because all drive around in Alfa Romeos.

All the states of the Soviet bloc present straightforward examples of bureaucratic tyranny, but it is arguable that other countries with more civilised traditions can avoid this fate, because their civil services often include some of the most cultivated and humane people in society, who are naturally inclined to resist improprieties, let alone barbarities. To such complacency, the awful example of Hitler's Germany is the complete antidote. The pre-Nazi Weimar Republic prided itself on being a *Rechtstaat*, that is one in which the bureaucracy was subject to an administrative law designed to check any abuse of its powers. The German civil service had high professional skills and ethical standards, and the longest unbroken administrative tradition in Europe. Max Weber, the great German sociologist, writing at the time with the German example firmly in mind, pronounced bureaucracy to be the most rational form of government though not economically the most efficient, because for him government was rational which made ever more precise through the rules under which it operated the principles of social organisation for which it stood. Optimistically he saw the continued growth of bureaucracy as part of the universal process of rationalising mankind. Yet the mental orderliness and attachment to rules of the German Civil Servants were their undoing. Hitler made sure that all his laws and regulations had a formal constitutional basis, such as his perfectly legal resort to emergency powers after the Reichstag fire – and then the functionaries became the creatures of his malevolent will. As Brian Chapman put it in his study of the police state: 'Conscientious, industrious and methodical bureaucrats were regarded as having become the instruments of mad, evil, and vicious men. It was like using a Rolls Royce not in order to carry passengers in comfort, but to run people down in the street.'[1] This is only the most alarming example in recent times of how a democracy which

---

[1] Brian Chapman, *The Police State*, Macmillan (Papermac), 1971, p. 56.

sports a large bureaucratic machine is peculiarly vulnerable to dictatorial takeover.

Plainly, the growth of bureaucracy constitutes a threat to free and democratic government. Officials may usurp the powers which they wield on behalf of the people's representatives. One characteristic of modern government is the growth of delegated legislation which gives extensive discretionary powers to officials, and, obviously, the more there is of such discretion the less there is of that liberty under the law which is the classic feature of a free society. Max Weber believed that the German people were politically stultified by Bismarck because he allowed officials to govern, but he hoped that organised political parties operating in a democratic parliament, and with the aid of their own party bureaucracies, would overcome the danger of rule by officialdom. As we have seen, when put to the test under the Weimar Republic, the theory did not work. The alarming constitutional feature of our times is indeed the way in which bureaucracies everywhere outgrow and overshadow the parliaments they serve.

Are institutional counterweights within the bureaucracy the answer? The French have their *droit administratif*, the British their ombudsman. Yet the auguries are not encouraging. It is a chilling thought, but it was essentially an administrative law set-up in Germany which crumpled under Hitler's assault. The example of Nazi Germany also shows that rival bureaucracies may do nothing to limit the abuse of power but merely make its use more arbitrary. Otherwise competing administrative authorities may simply bring chaos and inefficiency. In America, for example, the Federal Government's muddled pattern of administration and consequent erosion of authority and responsibility were criticised in the Hoover Commission Report of 1949. Apparently the main culprits were agencies which, though intended to provide independent reviews of administrative action, in practice only caused confusion.[1] Such examples tend to confirm common sense suspicions of the idea that the political problem presented by bureaucracy will be solved by creating more bureaux. For though competition to acquire sovereign power is essential to the health of an open society it is equally essential that in the wielding of that power there should be organisational monopoly.[2]

The latest fashion in administrative reform is the application of

[1] Martin Albrow, *Bureaucracy*, Macmillan (Papermac), 1971, p. 115.
[2] This does not rule out competition within the bureaucracy as advocated by William A. Niskanen in *Bureaucracy and Representative Government*, Aldine Atherton Inc., Chicago, 1971.

glamorous sounding new techniques – glamorous and new, that is, in the old world, but already old hat in California – such as systems analysis and programme budgeting. Unfortunately this sometimes translates itself into the bizarre application to social welfare problems of methods developed to deal with the complexities of the space programme. This procedure is often as germane as calling a hydraulic engineer to cure a coronary because his speciality is pumping systems.[1] It is a mistake to use engineering concepts in social contexts because, quite simply, people are not machines. But in origin the error was more venal than intellectual. Much of the propaganda for the systems approach to government was inspired by the commercial embarrassments of Californian aerospace companies faced with cutbacks in government contracts. Thus in the early 1960s they faced an urgent need to find alternative employment for cohorts of high-toned specialists. The public relations men were also aware of the commercial disadvantages of their companies being constantly portrayed as merchants of death and wished to demonstrate that the advanced techniques used in developing nuclear weaponry could also benefit mankind. Yet much of the work of the vaunted think-tanks has been worthless; some of the reports of the Hudson Institute to the American Office of Civil Defense were withheld from general dissemination because 'the reports were lacking in depth or sufficient value to warrant the loading of bookshelves'.[2]

Of much more concern is the peril to which democracy may find itself exposed by the cradle to the grave surveillance of the citizens by central government data banks. In earlier times the inability of big bureaucracy to digest the mass of information it possessed was some safeguard to the citizen. Improved card-indexing systems made the Gestapo chief Himmler's grip on Germany frightening by all previous standards, but that was child's play compared with what computers and data processors now make possible. Until now the degree of bureaucratic centralisation has been gauged by the number of bureaucrats; in future it may be possible to replace civil servants with computerised capital equipment. Thus as the bureaucracy dwindles in numbers its big brother propensities may grow. The privacy of the individual is already open to violation as never before in history. In Britain, the Association of Conservative Lawyers has urged the need for legislation to protect the citizen, both against government storage of incorrect or misleading data which

[1] Ida Hoos, *Systems Analysis in Social Policy*, IEA, 1969, p. 24.
[2] Hoos, *Systems Analysis in Social Policy*, p. 57.

is damaging to him, and against the improper divulgence of confidential information to civil servants. It urges restriction of official access to national data banks so that state servants can obtain only what is needed for the performance of their departmental duties.[1] Such updating of civil rights legislation is vital if we are to fend off the Orwellian state.

Exchanging men for computers, though it may augment efficiency in government, may at the same time make for government which is paternalist or even manipulative and despotic. The prime anxiety is that any restrictions a Parliament or Congress may place on the misuse of centralised computer and data power may be removed at a time of crisis, leaving the citizen more defenceless against the authorities than ever before. This is why the time-honoured attempt of libertarians to push back the boundaries of public power becomes currently more relevant not less. The alternative to the bureaucratic management of society remains profit management, as Von Mises announced to an unreceptive world a generation ago.[2] It is not the adoption of new techniques which will reduce the scale of government, but the revival of old and proven policies based on a belief in the spontaneous powers of people to serve their fellows while acting on their own behalf, as happens when we substitute markets for men. The task of scaling down government in the Anglo-Saxon countries alone is depressingly vast. Its accomplishment calls not merely for the expropriation of that giant expropriator, the state, and the restoration of nationalised assets to private ownership, though dramatic moves of this kind are everywhere overdue; there is also the need to eradicate a host of agencies designed to regulate, but usually acting to promote, the aims of special interest groups. Reform implies the elimination of tariffs and other kinds of protection, the removal of tax exemptions within a steeply rising progressive direct taxation structure, and their replacement by a much lower uniform proportional rate. It means, too, the abrogation of every unnecessary licensing system, for it is as true now as when Bagehot said it that 'the official hates the rude untrained public. He thinks they are stupid, ignorant, reckless – that they cannot tell their own interest – that they should have leave of the office before they do anything. Protection is the natural inborn creed of every official body; free trade is an extrinsic idea alien to its nature and hardly to be assimilated with life.'

[1] *Computers and Freedom,* Old Queen Street Paper, Conservative Research Department, 1968.
[2] Von. Mises, *Bureaucracy,* Yale University Press, 1944.

In Europe the most interesting question for the future is whether the Common Market will tend towards the increase of bureaucracy or the reverse. The present bureaucracy at Brussels, as was mentioned earlier, is minute, though it figures prominently in the demonology of anti-marketeers. Should the future emphasis of Community development be on freedom, as it is at present (for the Rome Treaty is primarily an instrument for promoting a free economy, providing as it does for the free movement of goods and the factors of production), then the tendency of the EEC will be to reduce the amount of bureaucracy at the national level. For example, if and when the various national fiscal policies are harmonised, the various national customs officials from the internal frontiers will be free to depart; or, again, a single European patent office will surely employ less functionaries than half a dozen national ones.

The European Community could, on the other hand, develop another way: towards protectionism, towards an inward-looking European science and technology policy which is the swinging modern version of protectionism. If such ideas prevailed, the Community would capitulate with increasing readiness to the federations of trade associations and trade unions which have already established their offices in Brussels, usually with a view to restoring on a European scale the protected national positions they have enjoyed heretofore. Happily, the continuing strength of Europe's balance of payments and, in a larger Community, the further liberalising pressures exerted by falling tariff barriers, should tip the balance towards a freer, less regulated, less bureaucratic society. In the longer run the most serious danger of bureaucratisation in Community Europe may come from attempts to go beyond the obligatory *harmonisation* of social policies, which merely requires them to be reconciled with a free competitive economic order, to actual unification and equalisation of benefits. This, if it occurred at all, would very likely be on the basis of accepting for the common policy the best, that is to say the most expensive, of each individual nation's social policies. As we have seen, public provision of welfare is, of all peacetime stimulants to bureaucratic growth, the most potent. We must therefore turn next to the welfare issue, looking at it in the British context. For it is in Britain that the clash between the two principal contending welfare doctrines, reflected as they are, if imperfectly, in the principal contending political parties, has produced the most passionate debate.

8

Service society versus welfare state

To those who think that the only genuine form of wealth is goods and who believe services to be either an inferior form of wealth or perhaps not even wealth at all, it is not surprising if social services should be comsidered not to lie strictly within the compass of economics. For instance, the statement often made by socialists that 'housing is a social service' implies not merely that the provision of housing should not be dictated by economics: the essential idea is that housing, which caters for a primary human need namely shelter, is not simply a matter of buying and selling, but a question of human rights. We have seen earlier, with regard to nationalisation, how economic issues can be bedevilled by the transfer into the economic field of what are strictly speaking political conceptions. In the case of nationalisation trouble arose through attempting to carry Rousseauesque political ideas about the general will into the organisation of industry. Similarly, in the present case, those who deny to social or any other services full wealth status cannot allow them to be dealt with in the economist's language of utility. So here there is a division: commercial services are labelled 'candyfloss', are described in fact in the language of non-utility and thus become candidates for persecution. Social services are, by contrast, promoted and extolled in the vocabulary of rights and privileges and political obligation.

The use of language inappropriate to the subject in hand is what Professor Gilbert Ryle in his, *The Concept of Mind* (Hutchinson, 1967) has called the 'category mistake'. It is a fertile source of error and misunderstanding. However, if we recognise the distinctive types of language used by the contending parties the current dispute over the welfare state falls into place. On the one side are the universalists like Professor Titmuss and his disciples, who wish to see everyone given free access, *as of right*, to a standard range of services continually growing in scope and quality and financed largely or entirely out of general taxation. On the other side are economists, mainly associated with the Institute of Economic Affairs, who, though also believing that welfare provision should expand, think that this should occur as a result of the expression of free choice by consumers in the market place. Their ideal would be to field the welfare state as a long stop with the bulk of welfare services being financed privately with the aid of insurance schemes to spread the risks.

It is illuminating that Professor Titmuss regards the use of communal services as the 'badge of citizenship'. The greater the dependence on the community evidently, the more prominent the badge and the more it must be a source of pride to the wearer. No doubt if the Professor had been a medieval knight he would have made his heraldic mark by displaying a begging bowl rampant on his coat of arms. The implication of his current argument is that welfare is something above price, beyond the reach of markets and not to be sullied by sordid commercial calculation. Welfare is to be wholly politicised and the scope of politics enormously enhanced. Logically pointing as it does towards the total socialisation of the national income, this is the most potent and insidious collectivist doctrine of the twentieth century.

We find the same pattern in the thinking of even a Conservative universalist who in his essential sympathies is far removed from Professor Titmuss. In his pamphlet, *The New Social Contract* (Conservative Political Centre, 1967) Sir Brandon Rhys Williams says: 'In a modern industrial nation which is also a Welfare State the individual and the community enter in effect, into a social contract, by which the group as a whole agree to dedicate a certain part of its total assets and energies to the provision of benefits for its members.' In return all 'should contribute out of their earnings that share which corresponds to the proportion of the total national product which is allocated to Welfare Services'. Here the language and political theory of Rousseau are bodily transferred into the twentieth century and dressed up in welfare garments. Yet the Rhys Williams scheme would, just as much as that of Professor Titmuss, make welfare a wholly political matter, despite the intention of hiving it off from politics, for welfare would be administered, not bought and sold. Changes in the pattern of welfare provision would be effected through political election not through consumer selection or defection.

Plainly, such welfare state theories, associated as they are with a lingering belief in the non-economic character of services, do not dovetail with the concept of a service society. Without rehearsing the general arguments of chapter 2, about the fully-fledged reality of the wealth which services represent, it is just as well to pause for a moment to reassure ourselves that welfare services are no whit less economic, no less a matter of pounds and pence than other services, such as banking, and no less intrinsically valuable to the community than the manufacture of steel ingots. Take hospital services, for example: many foreigners are prepared to pay, and pay handsomely, for the services of the London Clinic. To the extent that they do, the London Clinic is making a contribution to Britain's balance of payments every bit as real as that from the sale of Rolls Royce limousines; and who could doubt after the British postwar experience that any activity which contributes to the balance of payments is not merely valuable but positively invaluable! Yet many who would accept that medical services are marketable forms of wealth would still think of education as falling into a different category. As Dr West puts it:

> Sometimes the free market is objected to on the grounds that it is unthinkable to treat education as a commodity to be bought and sold – like soap. The confusion here is in the judgement of the vehicle by the things it carries. One might just as well object to the provision of schools by municipal organisation on the grounds that it is unthinkable to treat education as something that can be put on the rates – like refuse disposal.[1]

Linked as it is with an erroneous view of the economy, which misconceives the role of services, it should come as no surprise to learn that the welfare state is also historically obsolete. It belongs to the already fading era of the industrial state. As Peter Goldman has crisply put it, 'the Welfare State, as it exists today, is the delayed reaction to Victorian poverty and inter-war unemployment'.[2] It is certainly arguable that the breakdown of the traditional community based on the parish, the village and the municpality which resulted from the industrial revolution, called for the creation of something new to take over their social responsibilities. Industrialisation spawned a comparatively rootless proletariat which needed a paternalistic nanny-style state to teach its members to make provision against the hazards of the industrial system. Welfare legislation was needed to compel them to take such minimal steps of guarantee against future misfortune as to ensure that they should not become a charge upon the public purse.

[1] West, *Education and the State*, Institute of Economic Affairs, 1965, p. 63 n.
[2] P. Goldman, *The Future of the Welfare State*, Conservative Political Centre, 1958, p. 9.

However, the Welfare State all over the advanced world would never have achieved its present eminence on the basis of the insurance principle. First war and then inflation took a hand. The First World War wrecked the old liberal international economic order and subjected the workers to an unparalleled degree of economic insecurity which culminated in the 1930s slump. The Second World War completed the process. Much more of a total war than the first, it produced in all belligerent countries highly regimented economies, rationing and its corollary, state-guaranteed minimum living standards, together with stratospheric levels of taxation, especially of incomes. The regular habit of extortion was indeed the most enduring contribution of war because it raised the psychologically tolerable limits of tax which the people would accept. So when peace came and arms spending decreased it was possible to reduce taxes less than correspondingly and thus finance the mounting demands for state welfare.

In the meantime the inflations both of war and peace had all too often demolished the savings of the provident and created a universal demand for state security against the uncertainties or indeed the certainties of age, infirmity, sickness and family needs. Ironically the revolutionary and highly successful Keynesian cures for the worst scourge of the prewar years, namely unemployment, when applied to the quite different postwar situation only increased the rate of inflation. As Keynesianism also required low interest rates personal saving lost its appeal, while the Keynesian cure for inflation required the state to save on behalf of the individual by raising taxes. Everything therefore conspired to make the role of state welfare a rapidly growing one.

As the welfare monolith has grown its character has changed. In its early days it was concerned with providing for people in most need and insuring against the changes and chances of life. It grew haphazardly with the accidents of history. Yet the real change of character came, in Britain at least, with the advent of the Beveridge scheme for comprehensive social insurance, meant to comprehend practically all vicissitudes from the cot to the coffin. It was under the Beveridge umbrella that the welfare state became a veritable egalitarian engine, an infernal machine for redistribution. It was not so much a case of the majority of the middle classes not obtaining their share of the benefits – Professor Titmuss has lost much sleep in proving that the middle classes are as skilful at obtaining welfare benefits as one would expect them to be. It is rather that, first, the net effect is to transfer income from a top minority to the majority, and second, the transfer is effected according to a preconceived notion of justice. Such a system is unlikely to disappear with the growth of incomes, as some fervently hope. In practice the welfare state of universal benefits is no more given to withering away than the *apparat* of Communism. On the contrary it has a certain built-in tendency to hog more and more of the nation's income. So, to sum up the current dispute over the future of the welfare state again, it is between the enthusiasts for extending the existing universal system and those who would revert to the original conception of a state which is a support to those in need. The latter 'reactionaries' would allow the other existing activities of the welfare state to phase out in conjunction with a corresponding growth of private provision. At this point it is necessary to look more closely at the pros and cons of universalism in the developing service society.

The aim of the Beveridge scheme was the abolition of want, but this is the very respect in which it has been found wanting. Although social expenditure is now 25 per cent of the British national income the spectre of poverty still appears among the old, among the children in large families with low incomes, and among the chronic sick and disabled. The main reason is that state benefits are inadequate and have had to be reinforced by supplementary benefit. Yet it is known that many old age pensioners who would qualify for this benefit do not receive it. According to a Ministry of Social Security inquiry[1] over a million children were in families qualifying for family allowances but were in poverty all the same. About 160,000 families with roughly 500,000 children were disqualified from receiving supplementary benefit. This was either because their father was in full-time work or because he was subject to the so-called 'wage stop', a regulation which prevents an unemployed worker receiving more than he would if he was working.[2]

Among the symptoms of privation are the 1.75 million dwellings which the 1967 Ministry of Housing Survey classified as 'unfit for human habitation', the numerous bleak hospitals often over 100 years old, and the many gaunt primary schools.

These problems remain serious despite the very high and rapidly rising social expenditure. Plainly the resources are available for the virtual cure of poverty: the fault lies with the unselective system which in order to help those in need requires disproportionately greater expenditures on many others who are not in need. All at-

[1] *Circumstances of Families*, HMSO, 1967.
[2] These problems have been alleviated if not yet solved by Sir Keith Joseph's increases of cash benefits to the old and the chronic sick and the family incomes supplement.

tempts to cure poverty within this universalist system involves substantial overall increases in total public spending on welfare. Add to this the fact that there is no natural limit to the demand on many of the social services when they are supplied free. The potential expenditure by the health service on extending peoples' lives or on complicated transplant operations, for instance, is limitless. All this goes to raise the tax burden, which commonsense indicates is bad for incentives.

It is not really worth arguing the issue of whether higher taxes reduce incentives or not, any more than it is worth arguing about whether (other things being equal) people usually buy less of a commodity when the price goes up. Suffice it to say that the higher the level of taxation the more economic distortions and anomalies are produced because the higher the level, especially of personal tax, the larger the number of exceptions and special cases to be allowed for on grounds of equity. In particular, it is undeniable that high taxes foster the most wasteful use of service activities – for example, when top level accountancy brains are devoted to tax evasion because this is more productive in terms of net income for those who employ them than increasing productivity in works or offices. Through thus discouraging productive effort high taxes contribute to inflation. Colin Clark, who has found support in international statistics for the proposition that the higher the ratio of tax to national income the more rapid the rate of inflation – believes that an even more inflationary factor is the tendency of industrialists, under high taxation, to become careless about costs. There is also an insidious temptation to finance ministers where taxes are high and progressive to avoid restraining the economy when they should because the buoyancy of the revenue at least eases their purely budgetary problem.

Nor should we ignore the dangerous political consequences of a state welfare sector, gulping ever larger draughts of the nation's flow of income. The effect is progressively to rob the citizen of choice over the disposal of his income and transfer it to bureavucrats and politicians. Yet the failure of the universalist system to overcome the palpable privations of those it is peculiarly designed to aid evokes among some of its champions, the most petulant but also, surely, the most revealing outbursts. Take for instance the following pronouncement by Professor Brian Abel-Smith:

> It is not so much a question of public spending versus private spending but of whose private spending. Is the money better used enabling a mother of a large family to give children a standard of

living above a subsistence level or enabling people to attend Bunny clubs and gambling saloons? *This is the moral choice which any government has to make* (my italics).[1]

Notice the question is about 'enabling' different private people to do things. There is no certainty that the mother of a large family will spend any cash handouts on boosting her family's calorie intake. She may squander it in a gambling saloon. Nor will those who have funds which enable them to go bunny-hunting necessarily spend them in that hectic pursuit. They may choose to squander the money on books by Professors Titmuss and Abel-Smith. This is no mere quibble for the authoritarian implication becomes clear in the last sentence. This affirms that no limits can be set to the plunder of the taxpayer as long as Professor Abel-Smith's social priorities remain unfulfilled. So long as anyone has a disposable income which he chooses to spend on anything which Fabians consider naughty then that income must be forfeit to finance the activities Fabians think nice.

The public welfare services often tend to be remote and impersonal. The erstwhile doctor–patient relationship, for instance, has been superseded by a triangular wrangle in which the state acts as the paying agent on the patient's behalf. This arrangement seems clearly calculated to make the GP abandon his bedside manners. Admittedly this is just the British form of welfare payment. The method by which the state refunds the patient after he or she has paid the doctor's bill, as happens in some continental countries, would certainly help restore the old personal link. However, there is more to it than the manner of payment. There is the numbing effect of big bureaucracy which may well be made worse under the recent Joseph proposals to remove the supervision of the hospitals from the control of local authorities and place them under regional boards dominated by ministerial appointments.

According to some authors centralisation is justified on grounds of efficiency. Thus, for instance, V.N. George argues that 'the real cost of private insurance schemes to the community will be higher than the State scheme because of the higher administrative costs involved in running a variety of schemes by numerous insurance societies'.[2] Yet experience suggests that even if to begin with the state scheme's administration were ideal it would still, like all monopolies, deteriorate with the passage of time. The constant stimulus of competition from new methods and new techniques

---

[1] Brian Abel Smith, *Labour's Social Plans*, Fabian Tract 369, Dec. 1966, p. 12.
[2] *Social Security, Beveridge and After*, Routledge, 1968.

seems to be necessary to keep any organisation on its toes and keep the squanderbug at bay. In any event there is a more weighty political argument to consider. If there is to be a genuine insurance scheme for, say, pensions, and if the state runs it in such a way as to achieve a rate of return on its fund equal to that obtainable by private schemes, it will have to invest in equity shares. In that case the fund will quickly become an instrument for extensive nationalisation. It appears, therefore, that a national pension fund could only produce an investment income comparable with that of private funds on the one condition – a vastly greater concentration of economic power – which from the libertarian point of view is intolerable.

This critique of universalism in welfare would be very incomplete without referring to the vital issue of choice. A national monopoly of hospitals, for example, would be a much more serious threat to free choice as far as the average citizen is concerned than the National Coal Board's position as exclusive supplier of coal. Happily there is a small private sector in British hospitals which to some extent undermines the monopoly power of the National Health Service. Yet, according to public opinion surveys carried out by Mass Observation, most people would like to see this monopoly undermined still more. Even the near-monopoly in state education is now under fire on both sides of the Atlantic, especially from Professor Milton Friedman and his disciples. In Britain there is supposed to be freedom of parental choice. The 1944 Education Act laid down that 'so far as is compatible with the provision of efficient instruction and training and the avoidance of unreasonable public expenditure, pupils are to be educated in accordance with the wishes of their parents'. Yet in fact the freedom of the parent to choose between different state schools, even those within the same category, is severely limited by a zoning system. Only by following the most elaborate procedure, and by displaying great diplomatic skills in dealing with the Chief Education Officer, can a parent arrange for a child to attend a school other than that for which he or she is 'zoned'. Professor E.G. West has likened the parents' situation to that of people who are supplied with groceries 'free' (that is out of general taxation) 'but only at the shop nearest to them and any complaints to be handled by a "Chief Grocery Officer" by previous appointment'.[1]

R.H.S. Crossman who was the Labour Minister responsible for the social services is satisfied not only with the high level of public

---

[1] *Education and the State*, Institute of Economic Affairs, 1965.

spending but positively complacent about the rate at which it is growing. In his Herbert Morrison Memorial Lecture (June 1969) he proudly pointed out that the percentage increases in real cost between 1963–64 and 1967–68 had been housing 42 per cent, education 26 per cent, health and welfare 23 per cent, social security 29 per cent, and child care 31 per cent. Yet, as he admits, the fastest increase occurred in the last days of Harold Macmillan's premiership. The rise was not simply a result of Labour government: it is rather, he argues, an inescapable consequence of three implacable social forces which will inexorably go on pushing up the public costs of welfare far into the foreseeable future. These are demography, democratic equalisation and the advance of medical science. Let us examine these in turn.

The demographic argument is that the dependent members of the population, the young who are in full-time education, and the old in retirement, are becoming an ever larger proportion of a rising total. So the burden is bound to grow faster than the nation's income. Now this appears true, and if it is true it strengthens the case for matching state assistance with need. But population forecasting is a very treacherous subject in which the prophets have, historically, had a high failure rate. The development of biological science is likely to make future forecasts even more hazardous. Apparently there are 1,000 teams of scientists at work on gerontology (the study of ageing) in the United States alone. According to Dr Alex Comfort, the director of Britain's Medical Research Council Gerontology Group 'there is a real possibility of a breakthrough affecting either human vigour at high ages, or the human life span or both'. Again, in a lecture at the Royal College of Surgeons in 1966 Professor A.L. D'Abrell, an expert in open-heart surgery, told his audience that some of those present would probably live to the age of 180.[1]

At the other end of the scale the cost of education may be minimised by advances which are apparently likely in memory transfers. If biologists succeed in cracking the genetic code indeed it may one day be possible for babies to be born knowing as much as a Cambridge don, though, we must hope, also knowing better. Before that it may be possible to connect a pupil's brain to a computer during sleep and pump in learning painlessly. Aldous Huxley's Brave New World really is very much nearer than people realise. Yet even modest advances in the direction of prolonging age or computerised learning will make nonsense of Mr Crossman's predictions. Instead

[1] Gordon Rattray-Taylor, *The Biological Time Bomb* (Thames & Hudson, 1968); Panther, 1969, p. 99.

of a growing band of pensioners fastening themselves like so many old men of the sea on the diminishing number of active workers we may be faced by an expanding tribe of horribly active octo- and nonagenarians. Dr Adenauer was perhaps a portent of things to come. In the light of these very real possibilities Mr Crossman's proposals to saddle the Exchequer with halfpay pensions for those reaching sicty-five in 1992 were exceedingly premature. Meanwhile with the abolition of classrooms and lecturerooms and nearly all the paraphernalia of presentday learning, and the substitution say of a brief surgical operation, the national education bill may be reduced to practically nothing.

Mr Crossman's second pressure is the rising expectations of the workers. His belief is that the explosion of popular demand for consumer durables such as television sets, washing machines, refrigerators, cars and central heating, is succeeded by a surge of enthusiasm for better health, education and security in old age. This is very probably true, though the costs could be radically reduced by the prospective advances in biological knowledge just mentioned. Yet, assuming that the people hunger after more and more welfare, why should this require its public provision? As indicated earlier, the fact that welfare services are paid for out of general taxation constitutes a serious barrier to their expansion since it runs counter to the reluctance of the community to pay ever high taxes. Mr Crossman nowhere attempts to explain why the free market, which makes such a howling success of meeting the demand for a Bendix, must make way for the civil service when it comes to removing an appendix. Where rising expectations look for their fulfilment to bureaucracy they are indeed likely to go unfulfilled.

Finally Mr Crossman would have us believe that many services, especially in the medical field, create their own demand. He quotes the example of Kenneth Robinson, who was then Labour Minister of Health, deciding in 1965 to invest £1 million in developing equipment for treating patients with kidney disease, and that this service is now in extensive use. Yet, surely, all that has happened here is that there obviously was a demand for treatment of kidney disease, a demand which was frustrated because it could not be met without the capital expenditure of £1 million. In a free market some manufacturer or a national kidney hospital might have undertaken the expenditure (running a flag day to finance it) and then the demand would have developed just as it has to date, with the minister doing the deciding. The demand must have existed at the very beginning. For even a Labour minister would surely not invest £1 million in equipment for which he believed there was no demand at all. Certainly technology is, all the time, opening novel ways of fulfilling demands which are active or dormant in every sector of economic life. However, this is nothing more than a supply and demand problem which is continually being sorted out by the competitive pricing system. Mr Crossman's conclusion that 'there is no foreseeable limit on the social services which the Nation can reasonably require except the limit the Government imposes' only emphasises a problem which is bound to arise with any 'free' service in which ministers and civil servants have to act as agents for the cusomers and where there is allocation by administrative guesswork instead of by consumer choice.

What in essence is mistaken about universalist welfare is that it is welfare totally politicised, and as a result, insulated from the disciplines of economic life. For instance it has failed to concern itself, as it should if it were a strictly economic activity, with achieving the optimum allocation of the scarce means available for the noble end of alleviating poverty. It has instead become an illdefined pursuit of communal welfare in which the alleviation of poverty plays second fiddle to a gradual nationalisation of disposable income spurred on by the provision of 'free' services. For these the demand, lacking any economic limitation, is bounded only by nature (there are only so many teeth to be filled though there is plenty of further scope for fancy dentistry), or by administrative decision which may be merely capricious.

Assuredly the welfare state is not only concerned with the relief of poverty, though this should always be its first priority. It also has a duty to provide a guaranteed minimum of opportunity, an ideal which is best expressed in the educational system. Yet the political conception of education as a human right rather than a purchasable service is often in welfare terms counterproductive because it is at the root of many of the students' present discontents. As Peacock and Culyer have argued,[1] much of the trouble is caused by a distorted system of pricing and the case of university education illustrates this weakness which is common to all 'free' welfare arrangements. For a start universities considerably underprice their facilities so there is always excess demand. Of qualified candidates in 1966–67 only 62 per cent obtained university places. The result in terms of current welfare ideas is that 38 per cent are being denied their 'rights'. Meanwhile

[1] *Economic Aspects of Student Unrest*, Occasional Paper no. 26, Institute of Economic Affairs, 1969.

university service producers are in the happy position of being able to use other devices (than price) to limit demand, each quite naturally suited to their preferences rather than those of their customers. We thus have an institutional structure which constrains the producers to allocate educational resources in accordance with criteria far removed from those commonly thought efficient and desirable in other services and industries. It is the tension arising from those market conditions which constitutes much of the problem of student unrest.[1] It is true that in American private universities there is also student unrest but the tone was set by Berkeley where 'free' state provision is at its most generous.

It is not only that those conditions are calculated to upset the consumers (the students) who seek to exercise through elected bodies the power they cannot exert through the market. A further drawback is the source of the subsidy which maintains these uneconomic charges, for the gap is supplied by state funds channelled through the University Grants Committee. This body, guided by vague notions of social priority, exercises considerable influence on the courses offered, thus further reducing the students' choice. If all or most universities were to charge the full price for the services they provide, if the sole source of university revenues were fees, and if, scholarships apart, students were entirely financed out of loans, a market situation would be created where through the operation of supply and demand and competition many current tensions would be rationally and perhaps even happily resolved.

Few services suffer more from price distortion than housing. Yet it is taken as axiomatic by Mr Crossman and his aides that 'the private provision of houses at working-class rents is no longer a viable profit making enterprise'.[2] As a reference to the difficulties of the speculator who would like to put up houses for rent but who operates under a Socialist government the comment makes sense. As an assertion that most workers cannot afford to pay an economic rent for their homes it does not. Indeed such a view usually rests on a snapshot view of current income statistics which overlooks the significance of the family's life cycle. According to income statistics, many an elderly couple cannot afford to live in the house they actually dwell in even though they have finally paid off the mortgage. Rather more to the point is the fact that rent control and council house subsidy for over half a century have run down the country's housing stock and given rise to conditions which foster the illusion that the

[1] *Ibid.*, p. 15.
[2] Herbert Morrison, *Memorial Lecture.*

workers can only obtain housing they can afford from a kindly and indulgent public authority. Here again the return to cost and price realities is a *sine qua non* for cure. As others have pointed out, while there is certainly a problem of poverty in our society there is not a housing problem save of our own legislative making. There is no problem of supply of television sets though there would be if the government made a law that the prices at which they were to be sold should give the manufacturers no profit.

It is the deepseated belief that services, especially social services, do not properly belong within the economic order which is the root cause of these absurdities. An important step towards the reform of the welfare state is therefore to put the correct prices on the welfare services concerned and then attend to the problem of enabling the poor to pay for them. There should not be a housing problem so much as an inability of certain people to pay the rent. This is a useful simplification with which to begin. However, before proceeding to the final attack on the poverty question it is necessary to remove some misconceptions about selectivity being the simple answer to universalism. Selectivity as it is usually presented also suffers from the fault of dealing with many symptoms of poverty rather than poverty itself. This is very general but there are other objections of substance. For one thing selectivity, if it means dealing with every case on its merits, could be administratively more expensive than universality. For another thing it would probably increase the discretionary powers of the responsible officials. Finally, there is the danger that selectivity might be abused, and, instead of being a means of reducing state expenditure, may become a method of taxing the middle classes twice – once through general taxation to pay for the state service, and a second time when they are charged on using the service. It is the possibility of using selectivity as an additional instrument for the redistribution of income which has lately attracted the interest of some of Labour's left.

This array of objections certainly casts doubt on the feasibility of making a whole welfare system run according to the selectivity doctrine. Yet there is no question but that selectivity makes more humane and political sense as a principle, and that it works in particular instances. Thus differential rents and rent rebate schemes have enabled local authorities to concentrate rent subsidies on those council tenants who need them. At the same time a whole collection of *ad hoc* subsidies of this kind may be chaotic or anyway inequitable and indeed often is already For there are thousands of different means-tested welfare schemes (including those of local authorities which boost the total) operating in Britain. What is plainly needed is a method of concentrating help on those in need without a host of pettifogging regulations, means tests and inquisitions. At the same time the system should identify those requiring help automatically. It should not have such gaps as occur under the present scheme of supplementary benefits for which people must apply before they receive them.

One widely supported idea is that social benefits could be calculated by making everyone fill in a tax return. This would remove the strong emotive objections which attach to means testing. What could be more of a 'badge of citizenship' than the income tax return? What after all was the American War of Independence about if not that very principle? In any case the organisation for mulcting the citizen can patently be put into reverse for the payment of benefits. This is the so-called 'reverse income tax' which has been pioneered by Professor Milton Friedman of Chicago. There are numerous variations possible according to what importance is attached to complete adequacy of help to the poor on the one hand, and incentive to work on the other. The IEA Study Group on poverty came down in favour of a combination of a reverse income tax with a minimum income guarantee, by which the state makes up the whole of the difference between an income and the poverty line minimum. This proposal appears to be open to the objection advanced against the famous Speenhamland system which operated in England during the Napoleonic wars, that it would stimulate pauperism. The crucial difference is that, in contrast with Speenhamland days, Britain's poverty problem is now chiefly one of old people with very low private incomes. In these conditions incentive is hardly the prime consideration.

No doubt there are big problems. According to the Titmuss School they are practically insurmountable, though their gloomy conjectures are no grounds for refusing to experiment. Yet it is as well to recognise that opinion from this source, however technically expert, is highly biased and not only from a political point of view. For, as we have seen earlier, scholars have a vested interest in their stock of knowledge – their intellectual capital so to speak – and will do all they can to prolong its useful life. They thus become the most reactionary defenders of those institutional arrangements to the study of which they have devoted a large part of their lives.

Moreover, history shows how often the alleged experts are wrong Britain's PAYE scheme was brought in against the united opposition of the Inland Revenue mandarins. Yet technically PAYE has been a brilliant success.

All this is merely to allay the doubts. On the positive side there is the impressive fact that President Nixon has already put forward a 'Friedman type' reverse tax rate plan for families with children. The British may not be up to American standards in many economic matters, but in matters of taxation they are pretty sophisticated (if also a little foolish). So on this issue at least it should be possible to say, with confidence, that if it works in the United States, it should work in Britain too.

If the reverse income tax can put poverty into reverse the question remains: what chance is there of pushing back the frontiers of state welfare for the more prosperous remainder? Here again various studies by IEA authors suggest the lines of a solution. The general idea is to offer tax concessions on condition that people finance their own welfare privately. There is manifestly no problem about pensions. The present conditions for opting out of the state scheme must simply be made more equitable. For education there is the much more controversial proposal, again originating in the fertile mind of Professor Milton Friedman, that parents should annually receive education vouchers for each child equal in value to the cost of a state education. This voucher would be usable as a means of payment for education at any school state or private of required standard. Schools would be free to charge extra fees if they choose over and above the price of the voucher. (Logically, one presumes, schools should also be able to offer parents Green Shield stamps as an inducement.) The result would, it is argued, offer parents genuine choice in a competitive market and also allow society voluntarily to spend more on education without any increase in taxes. The proposal has been widely misunderstood and readily condemned in some cases because people dislike the word 'vouchers'. Indeed opponents, who are not always fully conversant with the actual proposals, often refer to them as 'coupons' implying, no doubt quite sincerely, that they would represent a return to wartime rationing. It may be that if instead of speaking of vouchers the authors spoke of educational 'credits', they would command greater attention and good will. For redolent as the word is of banking and financial probity it might command a more respectful hearing. It would also be more convincing if some studies were available of vouchers in action, though this deficiency will be remedied when the $5 million voucher project being launched in New England under the supervision of some Harvard educationists starts producing results.

Finally, since bad housing is a symptom of poverty and not a problem of supply, government provision of housing could disappear altogether. The restoration of a free market in housing is now well in its stride all over Western Europe. The socialist Swedes have abolished rent control. Even the dirigiste French now accept the principle that it is better to subsidise people than bricks and mortar.

The main objection to such denationalisation of welfare is that it would make no difference. For if those who contract out are compelled to purchase private welfare to an equivalent extent they will find themselves with the same disposable income as before. This is not in fact quite right because the opters will at least have saved the administrative cost of having a bureaucracy transfer money from one pocket to another. However, even if there is no financial saving at all, the changeover will be worth while, for choice would expand the resources channelled into welfare. Moreover, the growth of the welfare monolith is a menace to personal freedom. It is a gigantic organisation which, however benevolent its purposes, characteristically substitutes control and administrative decision for individual choice over a great area of the people's lives.

In any event this great welfare giant is out of tune with the times. In the developing service society as the theme is variety, so the political and economic imperatives are the diffusion of power. For unlike peace both welfare and liberty are supremely divisible.

9

Services for export

By one of the more confusing terminological conventions of economics the service element in earnings from abroad bears the label 'invisibles'. What exactly are these invisibles? The best authority puts it thus:

> The performance of a British play on Broadway, the shipping of foreign goods by a British vessel, accounting advice given to a foreign client, the insurance of a foreign factory, the raising of capital in London by a foreign borrower, the profit on a sale of rubber from Malaya to Russia by a British merchant, the purchase of British industrial know-how by a foreign firm; are all 'invisible' and all lead to the earning of exchange from foreigners.[1]

Yet their invisibility does not render them insubstantial. In 1968 world invisible exports amounted to $67,600 million – a round 26 per cent of the world trade total. Moreover, they have been growing faster than visibles for they were only 22.5 per cent of the total in 1952. Obviously, if this trend continues, in the course of time world trade will be like the iceberg of which the greater part is hidden from view. And among the suppliers of invisibles the Anglo-Saxons at present reign supreme. In absolute terms, the largest invisible exporter now is the United States with over a quarter of the total. Then comes the United Kingdom with 12 per cent which in relation to size is much more impressive and proportionately beats any other major nation. These two English-speaking countries between them provide nearly two-fifths of the world total. which prompts the thought that perhaps English is the *lingua franca* of the service society. The next, France, is well behind with 6.6 per cent and West Germany and Italy are close on her heels. The United States, Britain and Italy, are also consistent net creditors on this account; most of the others are net debtors, the main exceptions being Spain, who profitably sells her sun, Switzerland her snow and Norway and Holland their seamanship.

[1] *Britain's Invisible Earnings:* Report of the Committee on Invisible Exports. Thomas Skinner & Co., 1967, p. 11.

As to the components of international trade in invisibles, just under a third consists of transport and receipts from insurance of merchandise. Another fifth is travel and tourism and it is certainly the fastest growing, its value having risen nearly sevenfold between 1952 and 1968. Curiously enough the United States remains consistently at the top of this table, perhaps reflecting the old world's urge to retrace the footsteps of the Pilgrim Fathers and more verifiably the fact that visitors there tend to spend like Americans. A less American style of holiday spending arising from working-class affluence in Western Europe has, in recent years, led to a sensational rise of the earnings of Greece, Spain and Yugoslavia.

Investment income (28 per cent of the whole) has been growing slightly faster than invisible earnings as a whole. Here the Anglo-Americans leave all rivals standing with two-thirds of the world total in 1968, and it has been the United Kingdom's fastest growing item.

The remaining services (one fifth of the total) are a miscellany of such items as management fees, underwriters' commissions, film rentals and copyright, and patent royalties. The United Kingdom once had a clear lead over all competitors in this group, but now lies second to the United States.

Overall perhaps the most important trend, to which the original Committee on Invisible Exports was able to draw attention, was the increasing concentration of invisible receipts among the leading countries 'and the striking consistency of the surpluses and deficits, country by country, strongly suggest that the nature of invisibles (particularly the expertise they require) make them difficult to copy quickly'.[1] It is not, on the other hand, a trend which should cause any surprise for it is what earlier analysis would lead us to expect. If the mark of the advanced economy is the growing importance of services, then in world trade equally one should expect to find not merely that services are the fastest growing element but that the advanced countries tend to be most important in service transactions. However, this is only true if we include imports as well as exports, especially as some rather poor countries have a big tourist trade. A further distortion arises from size because the smaller the country, the larger external trade bulks as a proportion of national income. Thus it is not surprising to find the leading invisible exporters *per capita* in 1968 were Norway $514, Switzerland $309, Holland $211 and Denmark $189. Yet from any point of view the United Kingdom with $147 *per capita* as well as providing roughly

[1] *Ibid.*, p. 33.

one-seventh of total world invisible exports and absolutely ranking second only to America (which is economically ten times her size) was remarkable.

In the circumstances perhaps even more remarkable is the attitude of indifference or hostility to invisibles displayed until very recently by British politicians, and even British professional economists. As mentioned earlier, the official British view was summed up in the rule which was only changed on the eve of the 1970 general election, that the Queen's Award for exports could not be given to the exporter of a service.

This prejudice received accidental encouragement from the official statistics of British trade and from the way in which it has been customary to present them. It so happened that the merchandise trade statistics had, at least until recent revisions of unrecorded exports, the reputation of being very good, whereas detailed figures on invisibles were bad or unobtainable because until a few years ago there was little attempt to obtain them. As a result, it became the usual custom to present the invisible accounts as net figures. To make things worse, in the 1950s and 1960s, the government's growing expenditure abroad was deducted from the invisible surplus so that the net figure for all invisibles often appeared inconsequential. Political exhortations to export (not that these made much difference) were almost entirely addressed to the factories. The realisation that nearly two-fifths of British exports are invisibles has still not dawned on most MPs. Yet the visible trade account which attracts all eyes has been in surplus only in four years (1956, 1958, 1970 and 1971) since the war, whereas there has been an invisible surplus in every year without exception. This is indeed a very deep-seated characteristic of the British economy. From the time when records began in the seventeenth century and probably from much earlier, British merchandise trade was in deficit while the surplus on invisible earnings made up the difference. Only in nine out of the last 175 years has there been a trading surplus.[1] The publication of the Committee on Invisible Exports report on invisible earnings in October 1967 was undoubtedly a breakthrough, for it produced detailed figures on the exports and imports of the whole range of services which had never been available before. The lesson that invisibles matter was recently underlined by the balance of payments figures for 1970, for ironically it appears that invisibles, much more than manufactures (on which Labour's hopes for

---

[1]W.A.P. Marser, *Britain in Balance*, (Longman), 1971.

external recovery were pinned), proved to be the main beneficiaries of devaluation.[1]

Among Britain's services the financial ones seem to be unique. Let us forget the weary old controversy about whether it is worth while being the sterling area's banker of not; with the present scale of international credits ready to back sterling, the question has become academic. Let us rather consider how big a banking centre London has become. Even before the latest influx of American banks in hot pursuit of London's Eurodollars the square mile already contained far more banks than any other centre in the world. According to W.M. Clarke[2] in 1963 there were 98 foreign bank branches in London against 63 in New York, 48 in Paris, 25 in Frankfurt, 17 in Zurich, 16 in Brussels, 9 in Milan and 6 in Amsterdam. Since then they have multiplied exceedingly. Indeed by 1970 the numbers of foreign banks in London had risen to 159, and according to *The Banker* foreign banks are now coming to the City at a faster rate than ever before.

More striking still, London-based banks in 1963 had 4,300 branches of representative offices abroad. New York by contrast had only 182 overseas branches and half of them belonged to one bank the Chase Manhattan. London thus has an unrivalled worldwide network of financial connections, and one which could not quickly or easily be duplicated. Partly this is a matter of long established routines of behaviour which cannot be quickly copied. The same goes for that other great city institution, the Stock Exchange, business in which is enshrined in the motto 'My word is my bond!' That too has grown up over generations of business activity within a limited circle exercising great care over recruitment. There is little chance of its being reproduced from one day to another at another centre even if the necessary skills are available.

Another advantage is what economists generally call 'external economies', that is, the existence of readily available facilities where there is a large concentration of business activity, and it would appear that these are even more important in finance than manufacturing.

For instance, London has the world's largest and best gold market, the most important foreign exchange market, and, seemingly against all the odds, it accounts for half the liabilities and claims of

---

[1] In the bumper year 1971 the overall surplus of £952 million was made up of net earnings of £1,374 million on invisible account, £297 million on visible account, and a deficit of £719 million on the Government's account.
[2] *The City in the World Economy,* Institute of Economic Affairs, 1965, p. 12.

the Eurodollar market. This rather surprising development only serves to underline the potential of London as a capital market for Europe as a whole. For despite the exchange control regulations, London has managed to sell its expertise in the mobilisation of funds in various arrangements whereby the money is collected on the Continent in, say, Luxembourg, while the servicing of the whole operation is performed by a London merchant bank.

In addition there are over 500 insurance companies, British Commonwealth and foreign, including insurance brokers and Lloyd's underwriters and brokers. The general impression given is that the companies are rather more intelligent about their portfolio investments than about their insuring activities but, be that as it may, the fact remains that this is the largest international insurance market in the world. It is estimated that British companies pay out £1000 a minute all over the world in provident and marine claims.[1] Apart from all this there are many international commodity markets in copper, cocoa, grain, rubber, sugar, coffee, tin, lead, zinc and cattle food.

A further factor is the extent to which London acts as a clearing house for international transport. The Baltic Exchange is supposed to account for something like two-thirds of the free world's chartering of merchant ships.

To sum up, those intermediary and financial services which are the special province of the City of London make a formidable contribution to the health of the British balance of payments, amounting to £475–480 million in 1969.

In addition to these glamorous groups of services provided by the City, there are the more traditional types of invisible earnings which accrue from moving people and goods, though, even here, there is a growing non-traditional part of the market, namely transport by air. The widespread assumption, at least until recently, that invisible earnings had had their day was probably due to the changed international position of the British Shipping industry. The United Kingdom no longer has the world's largest merchant shipping fleet; she now trails behind Liberia and Japan. At the turn of the century Great Britain had 45 per cent of the world's shipping. In 1970 the proportion was only 11.5 per cent. No doubt the original overwhelming superiority could in the nature of things never last. Yet it is needlessly fatalistic to believe that such deterioration as has taken place was inevitable.

[1] W. M. Clarke, *The City in the World Economy*, Institute of Economic Affairs, 1965.

S.G. Sturmey in his classic study of British shipping[1] looked at all the usual explanations for its relative decline – the material damage inflicted by two world wars, the growth of protectionist devices such as flags of convenience, the rising costs of labour, the interwar shrinkage of world trade, interference by governments and unfavourable taxation treatment. None of these, he believed, taken singly or together, supplied a satisfying explanation. Rather he traced the decline to a defensive attitude in the industry, reflected in attempts to maintain its supremacy through various restrictionist devices which were generally opposed to innovation and the development of new techniques. Thus it was that the British became the chief organisers of liner conferences, devoted, especially in the years of shrinking trade between the two world wars, to freezing existing shares of the traffic. In the usual form of conference agreement, which is still with us, the members undertake to coordinate their activities and limit their sailings. Often there is a pooling agreement by which earnings on the trades covered are shared between member lines. All competition then ceases, for deferred rebates discourage the attempt by any company to increase its share while contracts with shippers provide a check to new entrants from outside the cartel. There is practically no incentive under this regime for any company to improve its ships or its service to customers. Over a generation and more it fostered an unadventurous spirit which militated against the adoption of new types of vessels. First the Norwegians and then the Greeks were allowed to achieve a commanding lead in the tanker trade. Again, it was the Norwegians who between the wars, adopted the larger, faster and more economic oil-fired tramp ship. British shipowners, and indeed shipbuilders, failed for many years to adopt standardisation of tramp bulk carriers, and tankers. All in all, the comparative decline of British shipping has reflected lack of enterprise by the shipowners and an apparatus of restrictions which they developed as if to institutionalise this lack of competitive thrust. For the liner conference system has in general a tendency to shield inefficiency, fetter enterprise and discourage growth. Above all it has been restraint of competition which accounts for the British shipping's descent from its erstwhile glory.

Nor is there much sign of these restrictive attitudes disappearing. On the contrary, it is in the most advanced, apparently thriving part of the trade, that the restriction has become most strongly entrenched. It was due to the initiative of the British P & O line that Australia/Europe Container Line, a giant consortium of British and

[1] S. G. Sturmey, *British Shipping and World Competition*, Athlone Press, 1962.

European lines, was formed in October 1969 to exploit the £1000 million a year Australian container ship trade. The consortium was to control fourteen big container ships which, with other equipment, represent an investment of between £100 and £150 million. These are to become a single fleet with integrated operations, pooled revenues and a single sales and marketing organisation in each country. The only safeguard against this combination having complete monopoly is the fact that the Scandinavians and the Russians have played out, but even they are within the same conference.

Similar restraints are at work in the airline business though here, if anything, the restrictions are the more severe for being the more effectively enforced. The International Air Transport Association, the cartel of the air, organises the most powerful international restrictive practice in the world. Embracing 104 airlines it maintains a resale price maintenance on all scheduled international air services. In other words, like the liner conferences, it fixes the fares and the frequencies of passenger flights. The result has been to reduce the world average passenger load factor – that is, the extent to which the plane's seating capacity is occupied – from 61.3 per cent in 1957 to 53.8 per cent in 1967. The British Consumer Council argued convincingly that an open rate situation on the North Atlantic routes would have led to higher load factors and lower operating costs. In support of this claim it pointed to the example of the Icelandic Air Lines (Loftleidir) which, while charging only slightly less than the IATA fare level, managed to maintain its load factors at above 70 per cent on its North Atlantic routes all the year round. The development of the whole West European economy appears to be held back by these restrictions, certainly in comparison with the United States, where fare levels are fixed by competition and are, as a result about 55 per cent lower, with a frequency which on many routes is so great as to create in effect an air bus service.

The odds are strong that the coming of the jumbo jets with their radically lower costs per passenger and with their enormous addition to available seating capacity must sharply lower airline charges. This could provide a suitable opportunity for a root and branch revision of the IATA system which in any case has lost much of the automatic official support that it once possessed. In the British case, IATA's restrictions have in the past only served to reinforce other restraints on competition arising from the entrenched semi-monopoly positions of the nationalised airlines which are strongly supported by the air licensing authorities. Fortunately this is now changing with the Conservative government's support for a second force free-enterprise airline and its adoption of a more liberal route licensing policy.

However, IATA will not drop its restrictions willingly or without a struggle, and will no doubt disregard for as long as is humanly possible the writing on the wall. At Lausanne in 1969 the IATA representatives failed to agree on standard fares for transatlantic flights. It was as well, for the big airline corporations had actually intended to raise them by 5 per cent. Their only concession was intended to be cut rates to people travelling in parties of forty or more, and this was only an attempt by the major scheduled airlines to claw back some of the business which had been lost to charter. The scheme broke down because the increasingly important charter airlines in the United States managed to persuade the Civil Aeronautics Board (CAB) that they needed protection. So the CAB witheld its approval of the new passenger fares. It was a happy example of the right thing happening for the wrong reasons.

The CAB indeed, like some other American supervisory agencies, has a dual personality. At home it steadfastly upholds the ethics of free enterprise and consumer sovereignty. Abroad it is crudely nationalist and protective towards entrenched American producer interests. Fortunately on this occasion American intransigence provoked European defiance. The Italians first invoked the contingency clause – which allowed them to cut other fares if the group fares did not go through – and were quickly followed by BOAC, Panam and TWA. The rate was continued until agreement was reached in Geneva in November 1970 to put fares up by around 5–10 per cent. This episode showed the increasing vulnerability of IATA's maintained fares structure.

It is still little realised that tourism is Britain's fourth most important currency earner, that indeed it earns more foreign currency than, for instance, the car industry which everyone thinks of as the spearhead of the British export drive. The selective employment tax, it goes without saying, was not a great help to tourism because it has fallen heavily on hotels and catering establishments. It will be recalled that when investment grants were substituted for investment allowances they were not available for hotels and restaurants. Having thus made these activities less profitable, and having made expansion more difficult, it was belatedly recognised that Great Britain was likely to miss out on the rapid growth of world tourism. At the behest of the Economic Development Committee for Hotels and Catering, the Labour Government therefore decided to make partial amends by offering loans for selected hotel development projects. Perhaps ministers felt that they had already done their bit for the industry by restricting to £50 the travel allowance of their fellow citizens going outside the sterling area, though the stimulus which this restriction gave to cheap package holidays abroad may actually have offset any surge in holidays at home.

It is in the group of miscellaneous service exports that one sees most clearly the value to the economy of activities which are still all too widely regarded as 'candy floss'. It is fascinating to discover that Sotheby's earn £45000 from their overseas sales of catalogues alone, that the United Kingdom sells abroad £20 million's worth of films and earns nearly £60 million in royalties, scientific, literary and artistic. Then there are the overseas earnings of a host of professions: advertisers, management consultants, accountants, solicitors, actuaries and surveyors, and in 1967 Britain's booming casinos brought in foreign earnings approaching £5 million.

The most controversial item in the invisible account is unquestionably overseas investment. British Socialists naturally feel there is something rather improper in the country's gaining from a rentier income. However, such delicacy of feeling did not prevent the then Prime Minister, Mr Harold Wilson, when the occasion arose from boasting to New York bankers about the extent of British investments overseas. On this matter, more than most, thinking is bedevilled by historical myth. Most British politicians probably still think that overseas investment income ceased to be important after the sales of our holdings in the First World War and even more in the Second. Certainly the total level of British investment abroad before the 1914–18 war at £4000 million was phenomenal. A clear indication of its significance at that time is given by comparing the net income from overseas interest and dividends of £188 million with merchandise imports of £692 million. Yet the greater part of those earnings was ploughed back into more investments abroad so that there was a rapidly expanding revolving fund. During the First World War £1000 million were sold off and inflation eroded the real value of the remainder, much of which consisted of fixed interest bonds. The nominal if not the real value of overseas investments was restored to £4000 million by 1939 but £1000 million were again sold during the conflict and disinvestment continued into the 1950s. In the meantime a debt of £3000 million – the so-called sterling balances – had been acquired during the war, not to mention the £2212 million borrowings by the Attlee government. Nothing daunted, overseas investment built up again during the late 1950s and went on at the rate of about £300 million a year until 1964 when it

rose to £406 million.[1] However, the timing proved unfortunate since
it coincided with a home investment boom, a rise in imports of
capital goods from abroad, and a general election in which the
balance of payments was the crucial issue.

According to the Committee on Invisible Exports' analysis, UK
income from overseas investments rose rapidly in the early 1960s
to over £450 million in 1965, but still represented only 1.5 per cent
of GNP against 8.5 per cent in 1913. British overseas investment
earnings have since continued to mount at an accelerating pace, for
the slightly different Board of Trade figure for net earnings by UK
investors overseas shows a jump from £400 million in 1965 to £581
million in 1968.[2]

There is little space here to enter into the controversy over the
Reddaway Report. This investigated private direct investment (as
opposed to investment in stocks and shares) which accounts for
£6000 million out of the £9400 million total. Suffice it to say that in
Reddaway's own view the most important result of his research in
this part of the field was that 'an average act of direct investment
overseas will strengthen the future balance of payments on current
account even after deducting the interest payable on the overseas
borrowing (or the equivalent) by which, at least from the national
point of view, such an investment is almost wholly financed'. On the
difficult issue of how far restriction on overseas investment is justi-
fiable he concluded that it may lead to 'an easing of cash problems
for a substantial number of years, but at the expense of making the
long-term problem worse'.[3]

The Labour Government decided to take the short-term and,
probably shortsighted, view of the question. Mr Callaghan's so-
called reform of corporation tax (which increased rather than decreased its complications) heavily penalised overseas earnings of
British companies. It also meant that many a double taxation agreement with a foreign country became a dead letter.

The main criticism must be that whatever the actual short-term
effect it built in an unwarranted long-term bias against overseas
investment. Further discrimination against the portfolio investor
overseas took the form of an enforced repatriation of 25 per cent of
the foreign exchange proceeds of the sale of a foreign holding.

From all this it is clear that Labour's war against overseas invest-

---

[1] *Britain's Invisible Earnings*, p. 169.
[2] *Board of Trade Journal*, 9 May 1969, updated.
[3] W. B. Reddaway, *et. al., Effects of U.K. Direct Investment Overseas*, Final Report
Cambridge University Press, 1968.

ment was not a phoney one. Obviously the long-term view is a difficult one for any government to take when it is beset by a chronic
balance of payments problem. However, the interest of a country
like the United Kingdom with her uniquely large twoway traffic in
capital investment must be against restriction. Apart from the
danger of stimulating reprisals there is a positive case. The flows
both ways are peculiarly beneficial. Not only, as the Reddaway report shows, do British overseas investments eventually strengthen
the balance of payments, but the inflow of capital which is mainly
from the United States brings in its train the application of a stream
of technological innovations from the world's most advanced economy, plus great managerial experience, the factor of production in
which the UK is currently most deficient.

The British interest in international liberalisation not only applies
to investments where it is shared with the world's richest nation, the
United States; it also applies to the other invisible items of trade
where the important trading partners are some of the poorest of
nations. Indeed, there is a danger that invisible trade faces a period
of rising protection. For the have-not countries are now seized of the
notion that they are not obtaining their rightful share of the often
lucrative international commerce in services. Thus the United Nations Conference on Trade and Development (UNCTAD) in May
1964 observed that the net deficit from services of the developing
countries represented three-quarters of their total deficit while their
own earnings from services amounted to only 60 per cent of what
they spent on them. UNCTAD therefore turned its attention to
ways of expanding developing countries' invisible income, and in
particular to shipping, commerce, tourism, and the transfer of
technology.

Certainly, as regards shipping, the developing countries have
some grievances worth nursing. Many of them built up their own
shipping industries after the war, partly to save foreign currency,
partly because they were unable to obtain the services they required
from the traditional maritime nations during the shipping shortage
after the war. Unfortunately the established shipping lines often
reacted to the new competition by attempting to exclude the new
arrivals from the liner conferences. This happened in the Indian
trades as well as in certain South American trades. In Nigeria there
were complaints that the West African Liner Conferences made
'calculated attempts to cripple the growth of indigenous shipping
lines'.[1] This discrimination has led to retaliation against the con-

[1] *Financial Times*, 14 July 1959, also quoted in Sturmey's *British Shipping*, p. 195.

ferences in the form of bilateral trade treaties containing restrictive shipping clauses. Thus the Conference system, far from furthering its primary aim of preserving the dominant position of established lines, may in the end have brought about a loss of trade. This only reinforces Mr Sturmey's indictment of the liner conference system quoted earlier.

Even so, it is questionable whether the developing countries will be wise in their own interests to follow chauvinistic policies towards international transport. The immediate benefits of restriction as usual are tangible and obvious: the more widely diffused damage less apparent but none the less real. Air services are an interesting case in point. IATA's resale price maintenance in air fares might be considered to be peculiarly helpful to the small financially not-very-robust airline, just as r.p.m. in retail distribution generally helps small shopkeepers. Consequently, the developing country with its own small airline, often acquired as a matter of status, can be expected to support IATA's high fares policy. Yet most of these countries have far more to gain from the growth of tourism which cheap fares are likely to promote. Happily the UNCTAD conference recognised this, and recommended that the 'Governments and organisations concerned with international travel, explore the possibilities for further reductions of passenger fares which will result in the promotion of tourist travel to developing countries'.[1]

But if there was here a glimpse of economic wisdom, glimpse is regrettably all it was. The wider lesson of the value, indeed the crucial role of services in economic development, is not likely to be learned as long as the prevailing development ideology holds sway. According to this, the unique route by which backward economics takes off into self-sustained growth is through industrialisation. It is thus commonly assumed that development can only occur through large-scale industrial investment either Soviet-style, forcing the community to save, or through massive injections of aid. Normally associated with this view is an attitude of considerable hostility to foreign trade. Foreign imports, except of such things as machine tools which equip the country for industrialisation, are classified with puritannical distaste as inessential. Thus countries like India, where the industrial approach to development holds official sway, invariably adopt rigidly protectionist trade policies, banning as dispensable luxuries practically all foreign wares which do not fall into the blessed category of investment goods. Naturally, aversion to trade goes hand in hand with hatred of all middlemen, who, in

[1] Quoted in *Britain's Invisible Earnings*, p. 227.

terms of the accepted doctrine, are unproductive and even parasitical. This is part of the reason why the Indian government had already nationalised important parts of their wholesale trade ten years ago, and much the same attitude lay behind Mrs Ghandi's more recent nationalisation of their banks.

No doubt this bias against commerce owes much to memories of the prewar depression when the terms of trade turned catastrophically against the world's raw material producers and by the same token in favour of the manufacturing economies of the West. It is not surprising if, even without any Marxist instruction, politicians in primary producing countries should come to regard international trade as a process of exploitation in which their own people have the unenviable role of hewers of wood and drawers of water. The Second World War added further cause for disenchantment with international trade, for during it many primary producers often could scarcely obtain manufactured goods at all. All of a sudden they were shocked to discover that their traditional suppliers of manufactures were blockaded or unable to deliver, either because of wartime shortages or because they could not spare the shipping. It is the simple interpretation of these experiences – that obtaining manufactures through trade is a mug's game – rather than because they are convinced of, say, the Rostow development theory which has led rulers of such countries as Australia into policies of accelerated industrialisation involving severe protection against foreign manufactures. Incidentally, the extension of the protectionist doctrine to coastal shipping must have done untold harm to Australian economic development. The regulation that all local sea transport between Australia's ports should be in ships manned exclusively by members of the Australian Seaman's Union meant that, for years, to ship goods between one Australian port and another was as costly as to ship them from Sydney to Southampton.[1]

The truth is that, contrary to fashionable development theory, the best way to progress is through free trade. This would be true even if theories that industrialisation is the unique highway to prosperity were valid. The economic history of Denmark shows how foreign trade is often the original source of an industry. For instance, Danish exports of dairy produce early prospered because the well educated Danes insisted on the highest production standards and imported the best equipment. From this it was only a matter of time before Denmark achieved her present outstanding place as manufacturer of all kinds of dairy machinery which she exports to over fifty coun-

[1] Colin Clark, *Australian Hopes and Fears*, Mouis and Carte, 1958.

tries. Again, Denmark's fishing fleet was at one time powered by marine engines from abroad. However, the service stations required for these gradually turned into fullblown marine engineers also with a worldwide export trade.

Nor is the stimulus of trade only of benefit to the relatively fortunate countries of Western Europe. East Africa's early development would scarcely have occurred at all without the Asian trader (or indeed without the Asian clerks, civil servants and professional men). In the early days of this century British administrators still appreciated this. Sir Harry Johnston wrote in 1902: 'To the British Indians I can only wish unlimited success since they. . .create trade, first in a small way and then in a large way, where no trade had hitherto existed.' Again Winston Churchill, whose considerable grasp of the commonsense of economics has been persistently underestimated, wrote in 1908: 'It is the Indian trader who, penetrating and maintaining himself in all sorts of places to which no white man would go and in which no white man could earn a living, has more than anyone else developed the early beginnings of trade and opened up the first slender means of communication.'[1] Sad to say such appreciation of the Asian middleman did not endure. In the last decades of the British colonial empire growing collectivism at home was reflected by an increasingly hostile attitude by colonial administrators towards private traders. In East Africa, Ghana, and many other territories state export monopolies over agricultural products and the licensing of traders became the order of the day, restricting business opportunities, politicising economic activity, diverting otherwise fruitful energies into currying favour with officialdom, and above all slowing down the movement from a subsistence to an exchange economy.

The long debate on European unity vividly illustrates the chronic obsession of Western policy thinking with manufactures to the neglect of services, as well as the influence of industrial corporatism the twentieth-century political doctrine, which, like old mercantilism, is linked with a belief in the economic primacy of manufactures.

It was significant that the first European community (ECSC) should have been organised to deal with the most solid, tangible and bulky of commodities, namely, coal and steel. Then the Spaak report, which provided the basis for the negotiations culminating

[1] This and the preceding quotation are from Professor P. Bauer's review of Dr J.S. Mangat's *A History of the Asians in East Africa 1886–1945* (Oxford University Press) in the *Spectator*, 25 October 1969.

in the Rome Treaty, found the main justification for European economic unity in the need for an adequate market for big industry. As it said:

> There is not a motor-car manufacturing firm in Europe which is big enough to take full advantage of the most powerful American machinery. No country on the Continent can build large air-liners without outside assistance. In the field of atomic science, the knowledge which has been acquired at great expense in several European countries equals only a small fraction of that which the United States is now putting freely at the disposal of its own industry and other countries.[1]

It is intriguing now to recall that the Common Market was originally sold to European public opinion with the glamour appeal of Euratom, the Common Market for Atomic Energy. Here the case was even more dictated by the belief that the future must lie with industry, organised on a continental scale, sustained by correspondingly grandiose investment in physical capital. With this big industry emphasis it is not surprising that in the Common Market, as in the Coal and Steel Community, the bureaucracy occupied a key position, for such is the logic of industrial corporatism. Big industry demands big government to deal with it and big government is incomplete without its complement of bureaucrats – or in this case Eurocrats. One must not, indeed, allow this interpretation to get out of hand. The whole eurocracy is only one-fifth of the British Ministry of Trade and Industry. Moreover, the innovation was at least negatively defensible. For if the Community was to integrate the corporatist states of Europe, it was with the national bureaucracies it would have to deal.

Again the Rome Treaty did not confine its attentions to industrial goods: it included ambitious programmes for the free movement of commercial and professional services, and the harmonisation of social services. Yet from the start the Common Market was sold to the public, both continental and British, on the big industry ticket, and that emphasis has remained until this day. It has been prominent in the debate on British membership. Of all the celebrated inadequacies of the February 1970 White Paper, which claimed to give a balanced assessment, the most striking was its treatment of the subject of invisible trade. After a sketchy outline of the factors involved it concluded that there would be a net loss on this account largely because of the obligation to allow free movement of capital.

[1] Spaak Report, Translation R. Mayne, Daedalus, Vol. 93, Izlinten 1964.

Admittedly, under a Labour government, bent on persecuting capitalists, capital flights could be expected, but even these would be limited by the small absorptive capacity of the pigmy size capital markets of the six. Moreover, as the *Economist* pointed out in a special Business Brief (24 July 1971), European funds should increasingly flow to the only European capital market comparable to Wall Street, and Europe's companies and financial institutions should increasingly tend to lodge their working balances to London.

It would also be reasonable to expect Britain's capital account to gain because it should tempt American investment destined for the Community area to concentrate in the one country where the natives speak English. It seems astonishing in retrospect that the 1970 White Paper made no attempt to forecast the increased export earnings of British services, despite the fact that these were the greatest contributors to the improvement in the balance of payments resulting from devaluation.

Provided the Community carries through its original design for the free movement of services and does not retreat into a new European protectionism, as the draft legislation on insurance regrettably does, Britain has much to gain, particularly in the financial services in which she reigns supreme. Even so the fate of Europe and Britain's place within it will not depend purely on what action Europeans take. The development of the service society is an international trend which European integration may hasten and European failure to integrate may retard but can never prevent. This is because the multinational company, the main instrument though which this great transformation is now taking effect is one which operates all over the world. It must be the next matter to claim our attention.

10

From international trade to multinational enterprise

The third largest producing unit in the world in 1980 after the USA and the USSR will be American subsidiaries abroad. That at least is what Jean Jacques Servan-Schreiber has asserted, characteristically assuming that American subsidiaries abroad can be treated as a unit.[1] Equally significant but less well known is the fact that the sales of subsidiaries of British, Dutch and Swiss companies in the United States are now roughly twice as large as the total exports to the US of their parent nations. Finally, to put things in perspective, in 1970 the world value of sales by foreign owned subsidiaries was at least $300 billion (of which American companies represented roughly three-fifths), which comfortably exceeded total exports of mercandise from major countries. This comparison graphically illustrates how far we have moved from the situation assumed by the neoclassical economists, under which the world economic order based on the nation state allowed goods to move freely across frontiers but not the factors of production. The old materialist bias of economics, with its excessive emphasis on goods, which we earlier decried, still prevails, and hinders recognition of this remarkable alteration of the world's economic structure. Indeed, in so far as it *is* recognised it is generally resented. In Western Europe politicians and intellectuals commonly regard American investment, especially by big corporations, as an alien invasion to be repulsed: in the underdeveloped world the usual view is that all Western enterprise is a form of neocolonialism. Here we shall argue that on the contrary the internationalisation of business deserves a universal welcome, for it is an agency not only for extending economic welfare, not only for completing the integration of common markets and common currency areas, but also for unifying economically the non-Communist world.

The international corporation is not new: it began its pilgrimage

[1] J.J. Servan-Schreiber, *The American Challenge*, Hamish Hamilton, 1968, p. 3.

at about the beginning of this century and it is fascinating to recall that at that time, when the first American investment caused alarm among Europeans a book called *The American Invaders* by F. A. McKenzie (The *Défi Américain* of its day) warned that Europe would be overwhelmed by the huge and rapidly growing production of American pig iron.[1]

The appearance in Europe, or for that matter in other continents, especially in South America, of subsidiaries of the American corporate giants was, in part, a natural further spatial extension of the national corporations which were already straddling the American continent by the 1890s. Yet at this stage European and especially British overseas enterprise was far more important than American. Indeed the American invasion was really in the nature of a counter-offensive, considering that in the late nineteenth century an estimated 15 per cent of the total investment in America was European. The European style of investment, however, was not usually direct. More often it took the form of bond issues by governments. It was not normal for large European corporations to develop raw materials, build railways, ports or electricity power plants through their subsidiaries – Unilever was important but not typical – instead bankers and financiers promoted mining, plantation, trading, and public utility companies for specific ventures, and offered their shares to the public. The major exception was the oil industry, for which geography, and the integrated character of its operations, conspired to create an international corporate existence.

The increasingly American character of international enterprise in this century has owed much to two world wars, after each of which the United States emerged as the largest, and for many years almost the only source of large-scale development finance. Increasingly, too, the international corporations have been manufacturing concerns, and even the oil companies have extended the range of their manufacturing activities. The reasons for this migration of American manufacturing enterprise in particular are tolerably plain. In technology and management the lead of American industry, apparent in so many directions, has made it possible for an overseas subsidiary to enjoy super profits for just as long as local manufacturers take to draw level. Huge marketing promotions incurred in developing the US home market for consumer goods yield products suitable for launching in another national market at little further cost. Jumbo size spending on technological research

[1] F.A. McKenzie, *The American Invaders*, Great Richards, 1902.

and development for the American market gives a company the chance to obtain a bonus through direct investment which mere licensing of patents alone could never achieve.

Again, international firms can juggle with differently priced land, labour, capital and enterprise all over the world and locate production according to the most profitable mix of these human and material resources. There are also tax advantages in being able to change the domicile where profits are earned. Yet according to Sidney E. Rolfe it is above all the antitrust laws at home which have propelled American companies abroad and, we might add, American arilines abroad which in more recent times have literally jet-propelled the world corporate top brass on their missions from subsidiary to subsidiary. Efficient global operations demand frequent face-to-face meetings between those who control them. It is not surprising then that the international corporations' most rapid period of growth has coincided with the most sensational acceleration in the speed of personal transport in modern times.

Commercial calculation alone thus explains why international corporations, and American corporations in particular, have advanced with giant strides in the period since the Second World War. Yet, if the corporations have been rational in going abroad, has 'abroad' been wise to accept them? In Western Europe, certainly, there is no lack of xenophobes who want the Americans out. Sometimes the reaction is merely comic, like the alliance of French Communists and wine interests who complained in the early postwar years of 'Coca-Cola imperialism'. It is amusing to recall that at about the same time the still more nationalistic, but also more adaptable Japanese were demonstrating in the streets of Tokyo with posters proclaiming 'Hurrah for democracy, boogie-woogie and hot dogs.' A more pontifical but essentially nationalist view has sprung from the feverish brain of M. Jean Jacques Servan-Schreiber in his portentous *Défi American*. Indeed, this work deserves scrutiny as the best argued and most influential intellectual assault on the American corporations in Europe. To judge by the words he uses, M. Jean Jacques Servan-Schreiber's approach is more that of a soldier than an economist; military phraseology abounds. Among his headings are 'The Assault on Europe', 'America's Arsenal', 'Battle of the Computers', and 'Counter Attack'. The phrases are important because the general staff mentality is that of the planner. Indeed, as Von Hayek has shown, the original source of contemporary economic planning doctrine was Prussia. One's impression is, unhappily, that though his outlook is liberal, human and generous

M. Servan-Schreiber, is from the beginning the victim of his colour-
ful vocabulary. Obsessed with his war analogy he is driven into
advocating policies both chauvinist and dirigiste. Let us examine
how this occurs.

The *Défi Americain* begins with the assertion that the European
economy is in a state of collapse; US business enterprise is in process
of conquering it. Servan-Schreiber admires the superior equipment,
organisation and training of the Americans which are bringing
them victory. Their brilliant technology enables them to dominate
those industries, like aerospace and computers, which not only
spearhead industrial advance but also set an enviable example of
rapid growth. The US technological ascendancy he, in common with
J.K. Galbraith, believes, rests mainly upon the sheer size of their
corporations, for he assumes that only the corporate giants can
afford to undertake the necessary expenditure on research and
development. Their size enables them to borrow cheaply and Servan
Schreiber regards it as supremely ironic that they are therefore able
more cheaply than their European rivals to borrow Eurodollars –
themselves the result of the USA's balance of payments deficit – in
order to finance their takeover of European companies. He alleges
that the huge scale of the multinationals, epitomised by General
Motors, which grosses more than the Dutch national income,
enables them to treat with European states on equal terms. They
shop around for government subsidies such as those given for
regional development, locate their investment with the highest
bidder, and declare their profits where tax is least onerous. He
portrays them as vampires draining Europe's best brains to America
where all the advanced work goes on, thus helping to widen the
already yawning technological gap between the two sides of the
Atlantic. He quotes with approval Mr Harold Wilson's warning that
Europeans will become technological helots in an Americanised
world. What is to be done? M. Servan-Schreiber urges his fellow
Europeans to create in their own society those conditions which are
the sources of America's economic strength. Educational investment
must have first priority, for only an educated democracy can
reproduce American dynamism or create its own independent
advanced technology. They must create an economic union, but
instead of relying on competition they must reinforce strong points,
namely the 50 or 100 firms likely to be the technological leaders in
their field (which are often unhappily labelled 'monopolies') and
foster their growth by mergers by tax concessions by the provision
of investment funds, development contracts and by other forms of

subsidy or near subsidy. Apart from that, Europeans must create a strong federal government comparable with the USA's, capable of pooling public procurement expenditures and therefore equally able to support giant companies in the crucial top technology sectors.

Servan-Schreiber's alarms are, however, ill-founded. The European economy, far from being in a state of collapse, is one of the most dynamic in the world; Europe's rate of growth *per capita* in the last decade has been one and a half times as fast as the American. Nor has his anxiety over the American takeover any solider basis. US corporate investment in Europe has been steadily falling since 1965, for the excellent reason that the rate of profit has been falling, which is itself surely an indication of the increasing competitiveness of rival firms in Europe. Despite their size, American firms have not been growing faster than European ones. Indeed, on the evidence of the last ten years there is no connection between size and growth as Stephen Hymer and Robert Rowthorn have shown in an international study.[1] The paradox is that both Europeans and Americans have felt threatened, the former because they look no further than the European Market and see only the American invasion, the latter because they regard the world as their oyster and see their global position threatened by the dynamic Europeans. Thus American corporate investment in Europe, far from being aggressive, has been essentially a defensive response by corporations which fear their place in the world league is slipping.

As for Servan-Schreiber's notion that the Americans are buying up Europe with funny money, i.e. with dollars that Europeans lend them, this is a latterday mercantilist fallacy. It is questionable whether there has been any real United States balance of payments deficit at all. Professor Kindleberger has argued convincingly [2] that the conventional definition of balance of payments disequilibrium is a faulty one. The dollar has in fact been strong, not weak. The apparent deficit is the result of joining together two money and capital markets with different liquidity preferences. America with a low liquidity preference borrows short and lends long and appears to have a balance of payments deficit. Europe with a high liquidity preference lends short and borrows long and appears to have a balance of payments surplus. Put another way, America's apparent deficit results from 'providing Europe with liquidity it cannot or

---

[1] *The International Corporation*, ed. C.P. Kindleberger, Massachusetts Institute of Technology Press, 1970.
[2] C.P. Kindleberger, *Europe and the Dollar*, Massachusetts Institute of Technology Press, 1966.

will not provide for itself"[1]

The power of the multinational corporation to flout the authority of the sovereign national state is less great than it has been made to appear. The multinationals seek profit above all. In its pursuit they may clash with unrealistic policies of governments, as when, for instance, they sell short a currency which is over valued, but in such a case they are only acting as the agents of those market forces with which sooner or later governments must come to terms. As Professor Harry Johnson has admirably said, discussion of this problem has tended in recent years 'to stress the obligations of the international corporation to enslave itself to the political sensitivities of the governments and politicians of the countries in which it operates, and far too little to concern itself with the limitations that governments should impose on themselves and their interventions in business if their countries are to keep the full benefits that the international corporations can bring them in the way of modern technology, efficient management, and the large-scale organisation of capital.'[2]

Almost certainly the American corporation have been the cheapest source of advanced technology available to Western Europe. Servan-Schreiber ardently believes more as an article of faith than as a conclusion from evidence that homegrown technology is best. It reminds one of Lionel Robbins's definition of a protectionist as one who fervently believes that home grown rhubarb is better than imported lemon.

No doubt the multinational corporation has as its political corollary the multinational state or common market. Yet it is perverse to regard European integration with its harmonisation of commercial laws and economic policies as primarily a response to the challenge of corporate invasion. It is more apt to see both as contributors to the same process. The multinationals, by striving for the most profitable combination of the available resources of manpower, capital, and brains, tend to equalise the rewards of these productive factors. Thus they complete the process which the mere free movement of goods and factors of production provided for in the Treaty of Rome could never achieve unaided. Servan-Schreiber's ideas of hurrying this process on through state-aided mergers would not have the effects he anticipates. Recent British experience is that only one merger in nine succeeds, and in America the success ratio is only

[1]C.P. Kindleberger, *ibid.*
[2]Harry Johnson, *International Economic Questions Facing Britain, the US and Canada in the 70s,* Britiah North American Committee, 3 June 1970.

one in four.[1] The main result of mergers is not more efficiency but more multinational companies, for past experience shows that size is a critical factor in the decision to establish a subsidiary abroad. This effort corresponds with what commonsense would suggest, namely, that the larger the firm the less of a strain on the budget of an overseas venture. The net result of the Servan-Schreiber programme, then, would be artificially to stimulate the further internalisation of business. Who knows, perhaps in the 1980s Senator Mike Mansfield will be treating Congress to startling revelations about the European challenge.

Finally, Servan-Schreiber's idea that Europe can be revivified through more higher education can only invite ribaldry after the French student revolution and associated worldwide follies, which stemmed directly from over-ambitious programmes of university expansion. It is in any case hard to take seriously an analysis which professes to discover the original dynamic of American Society on the playing fields of Berkeley.

To all who, like M. Servan-Schreiber, remain preoccupied with the American challenge, the Japanese example excites envy, even if it defies exact imitation: the Japanese uniquely combine extreme suspicion of the foreigner with an unsurpassed eagerness to learn from him. Indeed the history of modern Japan, ever since Admiral Perry with his black ships forced her to become part of the commercial civilisation of the West, has constantly exhibited this blatant mixture of hostility to outsiders with welcome for their ideas. Even the postwar American occupation could not change this dualism, but in many ways reinforced it. So it is that Japan, which has been the world's biggest importer of American technology is also of all the developed non-Communist nations the most free of American ownership and control. In the Japanese it seems the multinationals have found their match. Does Japan then furnish a model of what a policy of exclusion can accomplish, especially in view of her world-beating rate of economic growth to which this policy must surely have contributed?

It would be tempting to think so, as tempting as it would be wrong. On a closer view Japan demonstrates not the case for technological nationalism but its opposite. In the first place here is a standing repudiation of the case for a home-grown, and therefore independent, technology. For the Japanese expenditure on research and development (1.7 per cent of GNP in 1967) has been among the

---

[1] Christopher Tugendhat, *The Multinationals*, Eyre & Spottiswoode, 1971, p. 69.

lowest among all the advanced countries. Instead, Japanese firms have licensed technology from abroad, spending the staggering sum of $1460 million between 1950 and 1968.

In the second place Japan is now gradually removing the restrictions which previously prevented international companies from establishing themselves in any strength inside Japan, for, as the economy has grown, international companies have become increasingly reluctant to release their technology through licensing and demanded more direct participation in the Japanese home market. Japanese politicians and businessmen also have begun to realise that they can expect retaliation against their exports in the vital American market if they do not treat American companies more liberally. There is the further danger that the multinationals turned away from Japan will set up shop in Hong Kong, Taiwan and South Korea to the disadvantage of Japanese exports. Most interesting of all, the Japanese business community is coming round to the view that a more liberal attitude to foreign capital investment will introduce more competition into their highly protected home market; this should pep up Japanese industry and also benefit the Japanese consumer. Some businessmen even believe the arrival of the multinationals will help to reduce undue government intervention. They are probably right, for the most strenuous opponents of more liberal policies are the officials in the economic ministries.

So in all developed countries, including Japan, the multinational company is in process of becoming the main agent for the transfer of the techniques of economic progress. How far is this true in the case of the developing world? The most widely accepted view is that, even if there are economic benefits, the relationship is essentially one of exploitation, a view classically summed up by US Marine General Smedley in 1931:

> I helped make Mexico safe for American oil interests in 1914, I helped to make Haiti and Cuba a decent place for the National City Bank boys to collect revenues in. I helped purify Nicaragua for the international banking house of Brown Bros. . . . I helped to make Honduras 'right' for American fruit companies. Looking back on it, I might have given Al Capone a few hints.[1]

Exploitation, however, nearly always reflects monopoly power, and the Latin American example runs true to form. It was the domination of the market by American companies, frequently aggravated

[1] Ed. C.P. Kindleberger, *The International Corporation: a Symposium*, Massachusetts Institute of Technology Press.

by the support which the US government gave them when they came into conflict with local politicians, which created resentment. It is ironic nowadays to recall that, after the First World War, Latin American progressive favoured American and opposed European investment, largely on the grounds that the Europeans were associated with rural exports while Americans were more commonly involved in manufactures which were import substitutes. The American grip tightened during and immediately after the Second World War as the British position declined and that of the Germans and Italians totally collapsed. Moreover, manufacturers, lured by protective tariffs to make substitutes for imports, naturally found themselves in a far more intimate relationship with the authorities than the plantation and public utility enterprises which had been typical of the era of European investment. For their profit depended on the continuation of protectionist policies, as the home markets of those countries were usually too small to realise the full benefits of large scale production and therefore to compete with foreign products let alone compete in export markets.

The political situation in most Latin American countries favoured the growth of autarchy, with the break up of the old liberal international economic order, with gold-linked currencies, and free trade between manufacturing and raw material producing nations. The old conservative political structure ruled by landlords, soldiers and priests perished with it. In its place came populist demagogues like Péron, consistently under pressure to produce dramatic-looking economic results. It is not surprising that such regimes were ready victims to the hothouse theory of economic progress, that home-produced manufactures, stimulated by protection, would spearhead the development of a modern industrial economy. Greater economic self-sufficiency actually eroded their political independence. Tempting in American corporations was a policy reminiscent of the renaissance popes and princes, who thought they could solve their problems by calling in the French army, only to discover that they had started a process which led to the enslavement of all Italy. It is easy to see now that the Latin American countries would have been far freer of dollar imperialism if they had adopted a policy of free trade: nor are the virtues of free trade policy exhausted today, for it is precisely under the free trading dispensation that the multinational corporations can make their greatest contribution to development. The multinationals are more mobile than ever before, correspondingly more truly multinational, and therefore more readily disposed than formerly to manufacture components in developing countries, especially those which require labour-intensive methods. In this way there is a healthy expansion of the economy concerned through the growth of exports which are competitive in world markets.

The rulers of the underdeveloped countries would do well to take these considerations seriously and, in most cases, to revise their whole conception of an appropriate economic policy. The indication is that aid for development from governments and international organisations will contract, while that of private investment will expand, though, admittedly, the ratio of the public to the private contribution is still three to one.[1] Overwhelmingly those private funds come in the form of direct investment by international corporations. This has great advantages over public finance as a source of development funds. It is free of the political strings which governments often impose. It is equity capital and not debt, so that the country receiving it pays out in good times rather than bad. It also has numerous side effects. It brings in business talent of the kind which government aid programmes usually cannot obtain, because international corporations can pay the price and even more important can offer a career or choice of careers. It teaches skills to workers, knowledge and expertise to technicians, and the *mores* of competitive business to managers, and all this not only to staff in their own subsidiaries but also to their local suppliers. Moreover it has the organisation to distribute around the world and thus expand the country's exports.

In those parts of the world which are underdeveloped, just as much as in those which are sophisticated, the multinational company is thus the instrument through which economic realities are brought to bear on the policies of states. Only a foolish government will ignore its revelations. It is a happy thought that the multinational corporation, which has been so satanised in the past, is now increasingly the institution through which the facts of international economic life are being brought home to the underdeveloped countries. Truth will out, and, indeed from under the plethora of restrictions which shortsighted nationalist politicians have sought to impose on the pattern of commercial life, the spontaneous and widespread appearance of this remarkable free enterprise intitution, the multinational company, is a wonderful example of how inventive the unaided human response can be in the face of a genuine popular need. It is restating as a matter of fact rather than mere theory, and

[1] Rolfe, *The International Corporation*, p. 31.

in an altogether unexpected way, the old Adam Smith case for a free trade world. Instead of big business making a nonsense of classical competitive theory, which was always considered to be based on the assumption of a myriad small firms, it turns out that, allied to modern technology, and the latest communication systems the multinational corporation is the most powerful agency in the world today for global competition and confrontation of production costs. More than all the brain childs of politicians, it is cementing all the economies of the non-Communist territories into one world.

11

The politics of the service society

One theme that should have emerged in all the preceding chapters is that the economic policy of our time is dominated by a potent and mischievous myth: the myth, in essence, that there is a hierarchy in forms of wealth and that the great divide is between a meritocracy of wealth creation which is the manufacture of goods, and an undeserving helotry which is the provision of services. This dualism is implicit in the policy thinking even of those who would indignantly deny the proposition thus baldly stated. For the prejudice it manifests runs deep and is unfortunately compounded by the materialist bias of common sense. The prevalence of this distorted view of the economy largely accounts both for the inadequacy of the statistics on services and for the incapacity of existing economic technique to measure them with precision.

Would that this were merely a matter for intellectuals. Censure might then arouse some passing interest in the groves of Academe and even stimulate some textbook revisions, but no more. Unhappily the consequences of this error are more far-reaching and the interests vested in its nurture are well entrenched. For it forms the basis of a new collectivist doctrine, or rather of the renewal of a popular collectivist doctrine of the 1930s, that the state must be refashioned in the image of the large industrial corporation. Rejecting by implication the traditional democratic belief that power concentrations are iniquitous and ought to be diminished, the doctrine embodies a theory of countervailing power, according to which, as far as our economic institutions are concerned, one bad turn deserves another, and two wrongs make a right. So the cure for overmighty subjects is an even mightier state. Yet the diagnosis is as deficient as its factual foundation is faulty. Even in American industry the large corporation exerts nothing like the dominance that is universally assumed, and when due weight is given to the service sector which is larger than the industrial and which the corporations by no means control, the whole case falls to the ground.

Thomas Hobbes once alleged that the whole authority of the

Popes of Rome rested upon the mistranslation of Our Lord's pun on the name 'Peter' and the word 'rock'. However that may be, the mounting claims to economic authority of the new Leviathan rest in the main on the uncritical, confused and sometimes wantonly mistaken belief that 'industry' and 'economy' are, for practical purposes, the same word. So the new interventionist state generally favours large-scale industrial organisation and is for that reason benevolently disposed to monopolies, mergers and cartels. Indeed the reduction of competition seems to be its abiding aim. Its policy thus weakens the mainspring of the capitalist system as well as eroding the moral standing of the businessman, whose status, like that of a champion boxer, rests on the continual proof of his prowess by the defeat of all challengers.

Thus we have the paradox that many Western governments pursue interventionist policies in the belief that they are making valid responses to the growth of corporate power, whereas, in fact, where corporate power is growing it is mainly a tribute to the efficacy of interventionism itself. So, not for the first time in history, government policies are perversely bent on making false prophecies come true. The critics are right who say that corporate capitalism nurtures the seeds of its own destruction, and that the industrial corporation represents a step towards the socialisation of the economy. Marx himself observed that 'joint stock companies, and the diffusion of the capital of large undertakings among thousands of shareholders already constitute a destruction of private property'. Industrial corporatism is essentially businessman's socialism, not only because it undermines the property principle but because it also typically seeks to dethrone that other key institution of capitalism – the market. With its long-term contracts are fixed prices, its market-sharing, its exclusive agencies and limitations on entry of new firms and other restrictionist tricks, it is ever in search of ways to supersede market forces with administrative routines. No wonder it is ripe for nationalisation when the right political conditions arise. Before the 1964 general election the British steel industry expended much executive toil and even more shareholders' treasure in attempting to prevent its takeover by the state. Yet the ineradicable weakness of its case was that for a generation it had been an almost caricatural example of the kind of enterprise which is private rather than free. Like virtually all the other industries to be nationalised in Britain it was previously a cartel. It has taken the British business community a long time to learn (if it has learned) that the defence of private property in industry and the defence of the free market are indissolubly linked.

Those 'experts' who exaggerate the economic importance of the large corporations tend to make the economic order which these behemoths appear to dominate decidedly unappealing to the man in the street. For it is axiomatic that the bigger the organisation the more remote and impersonal it tends to be. Perhaps this is what was really at the back of Schumpeter's mind when he wrote of the rational and unheroic character of capitalism, its lack of romance and corresponding inability compared with other types of society to generate a sense of loyalty among its citizens. Of the industrialist and merchant Schumpeter says: 'There is surely no trace of mystic glamour about him which is what counts in the ruling of men. The Stock Exchange is a poor substitute for the Holy Grail.' The rhetoric is splendid but the argument is false. Did Schumpeter really believe that there is no mystic glamour about great wealth? The Stock Exchange was in any case a poor example to take, for no capitalist institution is so suffused with mystique. As for glamour it is largely the product of great riches. Where was there more romance than on the road of the merchants to Samarkand, to fabled Cathay, to the Levant, in the footsteps of Pizarro to Peru, to the Indian Islands of spice or mythical El Dorado? And what is it that gave and gives even the mention of these names their peculiar excitement, if not the lure of gold, the thought of wealth beyond the dreams of avarice? Recently through television's serialisation of *The Forsyte Saga,* the whole British nation has come to appreciate the romance of being a Victorian or Edwardian man of property. In our own century where has there been more glamour than in the works of wealth-obsessed Scott Fitzgerald? In his *The Great Gatsby* there is a revealing passage:

> 'She's got an indiscreet voice,' I remarked, 'It's full of . . .', I hesitated. ·
> 'Her voice is full of money,' he [Gatsby] said suddenly. That was it. I'd never understood before. It was full of money – that was the inexhaustible charm that rose and fell in it, the jingle of it, the cymbals' song of it. . . . High in a white palace the King's daughter, the golden girl. . . .'[1]

It may indeed be true that there is a deglamourising force at work in Western society which rubs off on to its politics, robbing democratic politicians of the charisma which great leadership requires. Yet whatever the influence it was strangely ineffective with the multi-

[1] F. Scott Fitzgerald, *The Great Gatsby* (1926). Penguin Books, p. 126.

millionaire Kennedy family, who brought to American politics a degree of high drama most of us would prefer to forswear. Still, the protesting students, hippies, football hooligans, and racial minority groups certainly point to some sort of alienation from and rejection of 'the system'. But surely they are protesting against a feature of the capitalist order which is not merely uncharacteristic but actually inimical to it? The deserved target of their ire is the bureaucracy of big organisations both corporate and governmental. They are unconsciously repeating in cruder terms the more lofty indictment of William H. Whyte whose admirable book *The Organisation Man* was an extended complaint against the increasing uniformity of behaviour and life style which corporate bodies impose on their executives, the persecution of talent and originality, and the consequent triumph of mediocrity in American corporations. It is not suprising if the humble as well as the gifted should see in these soulless corporate monsters a threat to their very identities.

Yet there is nothing inevitable about the corporate style of government. It is the deliberate creation of men misreading, often it would seem deliberately, that primary economic trend of our times which is leading to the supremacy of service activities. Indeed the modern corporate state is not only repulsive to libertarians, it is also decidedly out of date. It is truly, in Marx's phrase, a fetter on the forces or production, and nowhere is this more apparent than in the Soviet bloc, the ultimate expression of corporate government, which now faces mounting economic crises as it attempts, with corporate techniques, to grapple with the problems of the increasing sophistication of its economies. The Dubček revolution in Czechoslavakia, it is worth recalling, began with economic failure in what was in most ways the Eastern bloc's most advanced economy, a failure which was above all organisational. For the Czech economy, even after the reorganisation of 1968, consisted of a hundred large trusts, and Czechoslavakia still suffers, as do all the other Soviet countries – despite all the palaver about economic reform – from the evils of monopoly.

This is a message of hope not of despair, for the coming of the service society offers the opportunity to rehabilitate not only the philosophy of market freedom, but also the traditional belief in pluralist democracy. The dispersal of economic power to the twin capitalist institutions of private property and the market place appeals as much to the economist who deprecates the wastes of excessive centralisation as to the democrat who abhors the concentration of power. The demand for big government can only spring from a perverse misconstruing of events, for our times demand *responsive* government, and devolution is the first and most necessary step in that direction.

Applying the devolutionary principle has wide ramifications. It means, for instance, rejecting the industrial relations theory, rather fashionable, at least in Great Britain, that the ideal union arrangement is for every industry to have only one. Such union monoliths could be relied on to do all that is humanly possible to freeze the industry pattern, to resist especially the reduction of employment in declining parts of the industry sector, and thus hinder service growth. Indeed to make each industry the exclusive domain of one union might be the shortest cut to industrial stagnation, for it would establish in positions of unassailable strength the bodies with the most implacable determination to preserve the *status quo*. National wage bargaining on an industry wide basis already intensifies regional problems. The reason is plain – the greater the uniformity of wage levels throughout the country, the less the opportunity for workers in unfavourable locations to obtain employment by offering their services at lower prices. The whole burden of regional disadvantage thus comes to express itself in higher unemployment levels.

It is not surprising that the advocates of industrial unionism are invariably supporters of some form of incomes policy – that typically corporatist answer to the problem of inflation. In an attempt to impose some precision where ambiguity normally prevails, we may say that incomes policy exists wherever wages are subject to statutory assessment, allocation, and control. Its apologists rely heavily on the hypothesis that, in the post-Keynesian world, trades unions have the bargaining strength to push up wages almost regardless of the market situation. In consequence they contend that a central body is necessary to keep the claims within bounds. Yet such a 'solution' is a counsel of despair, for it feebly accepts monopoly in the labour market as a necessary evil: far better, surely, to devolve the process of wage determination and locate wage bargains at the level of the plant or the firm. The more completely this object can be achieved the more satisfactorily wage settlements through collective bargaining can be reached. There is, to be sure, a more vital issue at stake here than the machinery of wage settlements in Great Britain, for it raises anew the problem of power, Thus, on the one hand, incomes policy pundits pin their faith in the government or one of its agencies or creatures tirelessly resolving pay disputes like Solomon in all his glory, if not in all his wisdom. This is sometimes presented as an attempt to build up a body of case law comparable to the common law on wages, but the argument rests on a false analogy. Incomes are finally determined not in the scales of justice but in the balance of supply and demand.

In practice incomes policy merely leads to more arbitrary government. By contrast, the devolutionary plant bargaining school is usually associated with the demand for a framework of industrial law which will furnish some warrant that bargains will be kept. This has been a significant issue in Great Britain because British unions have but lately lost a position of immunity against the legal enforcement of the contracts into which they enter. So the clash of ideas over the future of British industrial relations, though the combatants are wearing different armour, turns out to be the classic confrontation between capricious authoritarianism and freedom under the law. It must be emphasised that the law/libertarian school is not hostile to unions. It wishes rather to strengthen their power to make effective bargains by confining legal immunity to employees who strike constitutionally, that is following the right procedure and acting properly through their unions rather than extending that immunity indiscriminately to all, including those wildcat strikers who for so long have been the bane of the British economy. Nor does logic demand that all unions under a devolved régime should be small. The crucial thing is that the bargaining should be local, not national. This change would leave ample scope for the union giants to provide technical, informational, legal and consultative services on tap to the negotiators who need them.

Such a flexible arrangement would be necessary even were the present sectoral balance of the economy to stay the same, but the advance of the service sector is constantly swelling the army of white-collar workers who, in general, take less kindly to unions than their blue-collar comrades. They are not so much new aristocrats of labour as an extension of the old bourgeoisie, and their devotion to the capitalist system is considerable. Even in large concerns they work in small human-scale groups, and are therefore less alienated from their work by the seeming remoteness and impersonality of the management than their more proletarian brethren on the shop floor. The natural tendency, then, is for the white-collar revolutionaries to support the capitalist establishment, for they normally identify with management interests and frown on mass action. If not left alone, however, if they find themselves in the sort of economic society where the prizes are poor, the prime object security and where only mass bargaining works, they may react by becoming much more militant and, because better organised, more effective in asserting their claims. The potential for social disruption of the white-collar workers once they begin to march is rather frightening.

On the European continent, between the wars, raging at the injustice of an inflation which had destroyed their savings they flocked into Fascist movements. Hitler drew his most ardent backers from among the petty middle class and it was a noticeable aim of the Nazis once in power to multiply the number of clerical posts in government ministries and agencies. This was perhaps the reason why the Third Reich displayed such a chaos of overlapping bureaucracies. In countries like modern Britain the choice of some groups of white-collar workers, especially in nationalised corporations, is to abandon the *mores* of the professions and embrace the bully boy ethics of mass militancy and proletarianisation. This is not a stable situation. Either the trend towards mass white-collar militancy must be reversed or the central government must assume draconian disciplinary powers. The happier choice from the standpoint of constitutional democracy is not difficult to discern.

If the white collar is then the sartorial symbol of the sector at present leading society's economic advance, some reservation would appear to be due in the case of the shopkeeper. It is not coincidence but a common hostility to economic progress which has in the past, led many small shopkeepers to make common cause with the more retrograde peasants, notably in France behind the rearguard action of Monsieur Poujade. The small, low-turnover shop appears to be the classic example of obsolete low-productivity enterprise. Yet the very emergence of the shop, that is the institution exclusively devoted to retailing as opposed to the craftsman's haphazard marketing of his own products, was historically a recent phenomenon and represented one of the most important advances in the division of labour which is proverbially the key to economic advance. Retailing essentially and indeed etymologically, consists in cutting goods down to the size, and making them available in the place and at the time convenient to the customer. The shop stands at the end of a long evolutionary development away from the household do-it-yourself economy, to the consumer-orientated market economies of the modern western world.

The impression that retailing is the dated Dickensian part of the modern economy owes much to historical accident. The enormous rise in manufacturing productivity associated with the industrial revolution stimulated few corresponding improvements in the efficiency of retailing until recent times, with but few exceptions, like the mass marketing of beer in Victorian London. So, though through the greater part of history economic development was largely shaped in the market place, by contrast the marketing both of the typical, mainly textile, products of the first industrial revolution, and of the more recent durable goods revolution reflected the economic ascendancy of the manufacturer. This ascendancy was always less complete than it looked but it was sufficient at different times to lend some plausibility to the belief of economists from Karl Marx to Galbraith that the market, and especially retailing (the final market outlet) could be ignored. Yet, for all their wiles, the advertisers who are supposed in the theory to be the satraps of a manufacturing hegemony know that poor products won't sell and no matter how impressive the promotion, the same fate awaits an Edsel as a bad banana.

It is ironic that the belief in the impotence of the retailer is so widespread at a time when the retailing sector is an increasingly dynamic feature of modern economies. The resurgence of the retailer was already beginning to gather momentum even a century ago, with the discovery by the cooperative movement of the economies of branch retailing and rationalised wholesaling, and the emergence of huge department stores, beginning in Paris and then spreading to big urban centres all over the world. But the significant changes have been more recent, with the coming, first of the variety chain store, and second and more portentously, of the supermarket. Both these institutions, by their ruthless pursuit of profit per linear foot of shelf space, by their exercise of massive buying power to squeeze manufacturers' costs, and by their relentless attempt to steal their rivals' customers, are gradually reasserting the consumer's sovereignty. The process was retarded everywhere in the postwar years by the system of restriction known as resale price maintenance. It is one of the most heartening developments of recent history, proving that the competitive ethic is far from being as dead as many economists would have us believe, that despite powerful lobbies dedicated to its preservation – for the Poujadists under other names were to be found everywhere – in every Western country r.p.m. now lies in ruins.

The materialist superstition that real wealth consists exclusively of goods reached its full flowering in the growth mania of the 1960s. It seemed at first as if the 1970s, beginning as they did with 1970 as Europe's Conservation year, would see greater sanity prevail. For the essential economic message of the ecologists was that we must not pursue material growth to the detriment of the free, or almost free, services of nature, such as clean air, and water, space to move about, and the beauties of the countryside. To the extent that this new concern over the human environment corrected the earlier blind pursuit of material gain the consequences could not be other than good. Unfortunately the more immediate danger is that our whole mental environment will be polluted with modish verbiage about pollution. Undoubtedly there are grave threats to man's very existence from a growing population pouring an increasing volume of waste into its surroundings. Yet this is no reason to adopt an attitude of mindless hostility to industrial civilisation. Even more mindless is the attempt to identify capitalism as the villain of the piece. A little patient enquiry reveals the countries of the Soviet bloc as apparently unable to learn from the experience of those nations which industrialised before them and, if anything, even more intent on despoiling their environment than their capitalist neighbours. Environmentalists in the West might reflect on this depressing fact, but generally they do not. Like so many idealists, most of them see little hope for improvement except through the adoption by governments of drastic regulative powers, to be wielded with scant regard for the rights of the citizen. Yet neither this draconian regulatory zeal nor the indifference which preceded it are what is wanted now. Instead, the issue must be considered as one falling within the scope of political compromise and economic rationality. Naturally it is not easy to reduce the boons of nature to pounds, dollars, or even roubles. Every commodity and every man, as Walpole said, may have his price. But what price a sunset, and how to value the rescue of the Scottish golden eagle from extinction?

The most promising approach seems to be that of attempting to define the citizen's rights to include access to an unpolluted environment and to leave the courts to maintain the balance between rival interests. Obviously this is more in tune with a free society than a barrage of government controls. It is manifestly better to proceed by extending the rule of law than by magnifying administrative discretion.

There is the further thought that, though many of the projections of the ecologists are needlessly alarmist, because they assume that man has little ability to adapt to scarcity and danger, they are right to remind us that the exploitation of the earth's resources has its physical limits. Yet the proper response to the recognition of this truth should not be an orgy of self-denial, but rather a reconsideration of human objectives. There is surely something false in the very conception of human progress as a swelling cascade of materials consumed, and material things to possess. True the pricing mechanism will of itself bring home the ecological facts of life, but there remains the need for reappraisal of what all this human striving is about, because the values of things are only in the end the reflections of human wants. Here, surely, the service society prospect is a heartening one, for it implies diminishing interest in guzzling and grabbing and new emphasis on economic activity, as consumer, in pursuing a higher quality of life; and, as producer, in ministering to the convenience and comfort of one's fellows. The typical promise of the service society, for instance, is not that everyone will have more electronic gadgets, but that the gadgetry will deliver to every home, at the touch of a button, all the treasures of knowledge and wisdom and artistic and moral perception of all the ages of civilisation. That is an inspiring, perhaps, even a frightening conception – can we afford so many millions of Dr Faustuses? – but it is not an ignoble one, not one to alienate the young, save for those, if such there be, overtaken by a sense of holy dread.

The revolution by which leisure is becoming the right of the masses and not, as formerly, the privilege of the few, is a connected question and raises parallel political issues. Among some progressives this development stimulates less rejoicing than despair. Almost to a man they bemoan the affluent society's vulgarity and materialism. Some, like Richard Hoggart, denounce it for destroying the old working-class neighbourhood culture, though in fact that culture was long ago doomed by urbanisation. Others like the socialist culture pundit Raymond Williams would put the media under the control of publicly accountable committees. Nearly all are paternalists when it comes to other people's leisure. Even more disquieting, politicians of many parties have discovered 'the problem of leisure', as if to say that leisure pursuits, whether cultural or sporting, need to be politicised. Here again, merely to enlarge the government's sphere of activities is not only naïve but dangerous, for it is likely to promote élitism among the political or cultural or media establishments, and the sense that they know best how the citizen's leisure should be spent. In other words, top people might be tempted to impose their own tastes on the masses, or indulge them at the expense of the masses in a sort of sublimated revival of the *ius primae noctis.*

If Great Britain is to avoid these dangers it is important to diminish the existing degree of monopoly in television and radio. At the local level every effort is needed to weaken the stranglehold of municipal authorities over the provision of sports and other recreational facilities and where they continue to hog these services, to require them to be more responsive to the users' or potential users' needs. And they are the more likely to do this the more commercial the criteria to which they must conform.

One patently uncommercial part of the service sector is the public domain, where bureaucrats dwell, ruled, not as the mass of mankind still is by the lure of profit, but by the law of that latterday prophet, Parkinson. For two generations now the bureaucratisation of the world has proceeded apace, hastened, not only by the conquests of Communism, but also by vaulting state expenditures in the democracies of the West. Many distinguished writers have observed this tendency and, not altogether unexpectedly, have found in it the march of history towards a predetermined socialist goal. There is, indeed, evidence that industrialisation and urbanisation have meant, for the public sector, a once for all growth, but recent statistics suggest that on both sides of the iron curtain the importance of state expenditure is starting to decline. However, that may be, the causal link between the stage of economic development of a society and the scale of state activity remains tenuous, and if an explanation of this lack of historical tidiness is required it is perhaps the obvious one, that all through history the growth of bureaucracy has resulted not simply from the play of impersonal forces but also, in any given state of those forces, from deliberate or casual human choice. Yet without slipping into the error of determinism we can say with some assurance that the main stimulants to collectivism in this century have been war and welfare. The present hope must be that, given a future in which peace carries on breaking out, given, that is, a sufficient sense of security for the cool reappraisal of western democracy's operative ideals, this stage of the service society is set for a gradual and (who knows?) perhaps even a dramatic retreat from collectivism.

There is not, currently, much commercialism about Britain's welfare state either, which is indeed one important thing that is wrong with it. This is not surprising because welfare services are commonly assumed to be beyond the reach of economic calculation. Welfare in the eyes of the Titmuss school is superior to wealth for it is the 'badge of citizenship'.

Yet the welfare state on the Beveridge pattern is already out of date in the service society. It is a postdated attempt to deal with Victorian poverty and the miseries of the great slump. It was justified in the period of the industrial state where it could provide a substitute for the responsibilities once shouldered by the traditional institutions of a preindustrial economy. Yet it seems certain that the welfare state would never have reached its present dimensions in Britain or anywhere else without the influences of war and inflation which destroyed the basis of private provision.

Unfortunately the complacent belief that the welfare state will wither away in the new conditions is not justified. The Beveridge universalist model, indeed, has a built-in tendency to swallow more and more of the national income. Even so it fails to cater for large numbers of people in need, including the old, the chronically sick, the disabled, young widows and the children of large families. It nevertheless exacts a heavy toll on the community in terms of weakened incentive, especially as the British tax system is so progressive in its incidence. This universalist style of state welfare provision is thus not only inefficient, it is also objectionable because it politicises welfare, creating a centralised juggernaut of standardised provision when what is increasingly in demand is more individualised welfare services, corresponding to the variety of consumer wants.

There will be no cure for this condition while welfare remains insulated from the normal disciplines of economic life. At present it is only subject to such disciplines as they are reflected through the distorted mirrors of state necessity and bureaucratic convenience. If welfare arrangements are to fulfil the twin aims of relieving poverty and providing minimum opportunity, welfare must become once again a part of a rational economic order. Welfare services must bear the right price tabs, must be subject to the stimulus and discipline of competition, and should, wherever possible, be bought and sold rather than allocated and administered. Then the problem becomes one of ensuring that the poor can pay for them. On balance the best way to arrange this appears not to be through a collection of *ad hoc* selective services, because this is too complicated and may miss out many people in distress: more hopeful is the idea of a minimum income guarantee, together with (and here we take a leaf out of President Nixon's book) a reverse income tax. Though there is much in detail to consider about this reform, the bold approach to the essential problem of need is very appealing.

The essential argument of this book, the threads of which we have just brought together is, it is true, out of sympathy with fashionable 'liberal' corporatist assumptions of western policy makers, their advisers, and their academic apologists. The conventional wisdom against which J.K. Galbraith inveighs with such affluent rhetoric is, in Britain at least, massed on his side. Indeed, as a recent Reith lecturer and current fellow of King's College, Cambridge, Galbraith rates as a fully paid-up member of the trendy establishment. In earlier times the current intellectual drift to collectivism might not have mattered, for fashions in political and economic thinking rise and fall like hemlines if not so frequently. Unfortunately the Galbraithian type arguments in favour of greater concentration of state power come at a time when science is opening up opportunities to make that concentration permanent. It is significant that Aldous Huxley and George Orwell should both have conceived a future human society shaped by science and technology as a dictatorship. The only difference between the time when they wrote and now is that the dangers are much nearer. The present capacity for electronic surveillance already makes the big brother government of 1984 look perfectly feasible. Brain washing, again, has made great strides since Huxley envisaged infants being indoctrinated in their sleep by gramophones playing under their pillows. Developments in drugs enhance the possibility of mood control perhaps of whole populations. Huxley's 'soma' may soon be synthesised. The first steps towards test-tube babies are even now being made. Advances in the study of microbiology may soon lead to the cracking of the genetic code. Tinkering with heredity is apparently on the agenda in the next ten or twenty years, and subject people with, say, passive nonrevolutionary characteristics may be made to order.

Concentration of power is thus more dangerous than in the past because science may strengthen the hands of the authorities over their subjects as never before in history. The damaging effect of the Galbraithian myth is that it induces people to believe that this gathering of power into fewer and fewer hands is inevitable, and that it is fruitless to try to oppose it. The intention here has been to show that on the contrary, far from urging us towards more centralised government, the most fundamental economic trend of our time, which is towards the growth of services, actually favours power dispersal. In so far as centralisation continues, it is the product of policies and laws which we may change if we choose. It cannot be too much emphasised that, of itself, the service economy is a sounder foundation for a liberal capitalist social order than the predominantly industrial economy which, historically, precedes it. The affluent capitalism of the service economy is, paradoxically, also more compatible with ideas of social democracy than earlier stages of economic development. It is likely to be less hierarchical. Status will be less based upon heredity because property income will be a smaller and smaller fraction of total national income, while the fraction representing the earnings of human services will continue to grow.

This point is missed entirely in the otherwise perceptive and entertaining satire by Michael Young, *The Rise of Meritocracy* (Thames and Hudson, 1961). He foresees the unskilled workers everywhere being displaced by machines. As a result they will be good for nothing but domestic service. So the low IQ people will finish up waiting on the members of Mensa, that is the upper crust chosen for their high IQs. The hierarchical Victorian household plus the snobbish Victorian society will be resurrected. Civilisation will thus move backwards from contract to status; away from cash nexus and back to caste, rank and title. Yet, though ingenious, this interpretation misreads the economic auguries. More personal services there will be, but, increasingly, these will be contractual. The real pattern of the future is shown by the fact that Oxford colleges – surely the most tradition-bound and hierarchical of British institutions – are more and more having their meals in hall provided by contract caterers, their lawns mown and their flower beds tended by contract gardeners. This development offers ample opportunity to people of humble abilities to develop into self-confident entrepreneurs providing contract services, in contrast with the forelock-touching· menials of yesteryear.

If the politics of Western countries are wantonly burdened with a damaging myth, at least it is possible to abandon those corporatist policies which are founded on it. The main embarrassments are what might be described as 'nature's conservatives', those who believe the essence of political wisdom is to keep things as they are, who can envisage no state better than the *status quo*, and no social goal more worth pursuing than the perpetuation of the present. Yet their hope of immobility rests on an ancient illusion. Even Heraclitus knew that we never step into the same river twice. The politics of consolidation are fatal to true conservatism at a time when, as in Britain, the enemy seeks to undermine the very foundations of society. For consolidation is no more than the prelude to further retreat, a process which continues until the citadel has fallen and there is nothing left to defend. At such times true conservatism calls not for inaction but for an aggressive radicalism aiming not merely to arrest history when it is moving the wrong way but to urge it into reverse. When there is a Gadarene rush the argument is overwhelmingly in favour of reaction.

Many Conservatives have been deceived by another metaphor much employed by public opinion analysts – that of the 'middle ground' which they are advised to contest with their opponents. The effect of this is usually the acceptance of a consensus which is imposed by the other side. This was what classically happened in the later years of Mr Harold Macmillan's government in Britain. Mr Macmillan was a believer in the middle way. The fate of his party was predictable. 'You know what happens to people who stand in the middle of the road?' said his old opponent Aneurin Bevan – 'They get run over.'

Britain, more, probably, than any other Western country, stands in need of a conservatism of the radical variety. British Conservatives had already been warned by Mr Marsh, the minister then responsible, that Labour's nationalisation of steel was so arranged that it would be impossible to denationalise again. Those who think that sensible compromise is achievable on this issue should ponder that cynical assurance. What is called for is not simple reversal but an operative ideal of how to establish, on a more permanent basis, the political economy of freedom.

Some working theory is necessary to apply to, for instance, the thorny problems of denationalisation. In this respect British Conservatives, never very much at home with political theory, have been a disadvantage. Over the years pragmatism served them well. Principles were until recently unfashionable, doctrine at a discount. The essential thing was to hold power. Yet if in this way they were successful in containing their opponents, it was success bought at a price. And that price was the acceptance of the Beveridge scheme of universal welfare, and latterly a further leftward lurch in the economic policy consensus to include planning, incomes policy and modernisation through high public spending. However, the election of Edward Heath as leader signalled the arrival of a more robust style of conservatism. For he it was who had instigated the repeal of resale price maintenance, the only major legislative move towards stiffer competition during the final spell of Conservative government, and an unpopular one among some of the most vocal Conservative supporters. The combination of Edward Heath's leadership with the party's unaccustomed deprivation of the sweets of office resulted, not before time, in some plainer living and higher thinking. The diffident consent to left-inclined consensus yielded to an emphasis on the great divide, and the search for a practical antithesis to socialism. A similar toughening of mood is appearing among President Nixon's Republicans. Progressives instinctively reach for the blanket term 'backlash'. Yet there is reason to hope that there is actually emerging a new more coherent philosophy of the right, which provides the basis of a political counteroffensive.

It is long overdue. For half a century and more, working theories of revolution have been in ample supply. Marxists have never lost the analytical British Museum library approach of their founder, and observe every society like surgeons preparing for an operation, distinguishing the centres of power, the points of weakness, the classes and often small groups which hold the keys to the potential coup d'état. Herbert Marcuse's irrationalist rantings and pseudophilosophical mumbo-jumbo should not blind us to the acute underlying analysis of the techniques of subversion including – in anthentic Nazi style – the calculated use of obscenity against the authorities.[1]

What is now starting to appear is the same calculation applied to the defence of freedom and order. Sir Karl Popper talks of 'piecemeal social engineering' as the role of politicians in a liberal democracy. The phrase is unattractive, but it may serve to remind us that building the bulwarks of liberty is not a haphazard activity to be left entirely to chance. Admittedly, the unique strength of a free society is its power of spontaneous response. Yet certain conditions are more favourable to spontaneity than others. For instance, it is futile to expect businessmen to display heroic enterprise within a regime of rigid price control – not that any feeling of unfairness or inconsistency has ever restrained political critics of free enterprise from blaming its failure to perform when they themselves have ensured its paralysis!

In enumerating the conditions necessary for the harmonious development of the service economy, the most advanced yet known to man, the first and most obvious is the avoidance of competitive distortions by such fiscal absurdities as the British selective employment tax. Yet this is only the beginning of the process of revising all the arrangements which falsify the effects of competition in the service sector. In Great Britain one has only to look at the severe restrictions on hours of opening, or on entry of newcomers, through licensing and other means, which afflict the great spread of services represented by shops, pubs, banks, and taxis, to appreciate the immense programme of reform which the introduction of free competition represents.[2] With this must go a loosening up of the conditions of employment to involve the jettisoning of rigid hours. For these work against the performance of part time jobs by women and old people, which commonsense and the convenience of the service consumer and producer alike prescribe as the pattern of the future.

The same line of reasoning has already, in the British case, brought

[1] Herbert Marcuse, *An Essay on Liberation*, Allen Lane, 1969, p. 35.
[2] See the author's *Bonfire of Restrictions*, Conservative Political Centre, 1965.

the dismantling of three agencies of industrial corporatism, namely the Land Commission, the Industrial Reorganisation Corporation (which is, of all Labour's creations, the body most directly inspired by the institutional fall-out from Fascist Italy), and the Prices and Incomes Board. Yet few matters are more crucial for the fate of free institutions in Britain than that success should attend the next stage in dethroning collectivism to wit denationalisation – the most explicit repudiation possible of industrial corporatism, and a process which must in future be viewed as a means of consolidating a peaceful counterrevolution rather than as an awkward moment in the history of the capital issue market. If it is to win through it must be linked with a grand design for popular capitalism. If the pushing back of the frontiers of public ownership is to be more than a brief sortie with no lasting influence on the war, it must consolidate itself on the self-interest of a million small investors. The service society must be seen to serve the multitudes. Indeed, if western democracy is to survive, all its economic arrangements need to be reappraised with the object of removing artificial and irrational barriers (whether fiscal, bureaucratic, legalistic or monopolistic) to the dispersal of ownership and the widespread revival of the propensity to save. Unfortunately Keynes made personal saving the arch-delinquent of the depression drama, criminally responsible for the impotence of effective demand, and it is only slowly reestablishing its claim to be the source of economic virility. In order now to restore fully the popular willingness to save, it may be necessary, for a time at least, to give what might appear to be inequitable boons to small savers, for what is at stake is the integrity of the social fabric.

Yet if personal saving is to be reinstated to its former glory it is a clear corollary that state saving should decline correspondingly. The main implication is a massive conversion of state welfare into welfare privately provided and financed. There seems to be no insuperable difficulty in practice. State welfare can become smaller in scale through being selective, while the boldest, most appealing approach to selectivity is through the use of a reverse income tax combined with a minimum income guarantee. Beyond this, existing state schemes can be extensively denationalised through fiscal incentives, or at least the removal of disincentives to contract out.

There remains a problem which is likely to loom larger as the service economy becomes more pervasive. This is the tendency for all kinds of charitable trusts to be established creating foundations for health, recreation, scientific research and so on, which are mostly the fruits of resoundingly successful entrepreneurial careers. In earlier times these tycoons would have left the money to provide for masses to be said for their souls: nowadays they finance other, perhaps equally dedicated, secular offerings. The paradox is that these bodies normally do not need to pursue profit because, almost regardless of what they do, the foundation will provide. This could lead to a vast wastage of resources, for without profit as a measure of the use to which they put them the managers will often have no idea whether they are using the funds they control in a rational fashion or not. This is the most alarming exception to the otherwise justified generalisation that a service-dominated economy is peculiarly suited to the operation of the system of competitive capitalism. Not that the matter can be left there. Surely, until some alternative criterion to the maximisation of profit is invented, which can serve as a guide to the best way to run an organisation, the aim should be to find methods of reintroducing profit as a standard of performance into the calculations of the trustees. Otherwise the service society may, in the medium term, provide the setting for the rehabilitation of the market economy, but in the long run be socialised, just as Schumpeter said it would be, paradoxically, by its own success. As the worldwide production and consumption of services overtakes that of goods, so service transactions, known as 'invisibles' and currently a quarter of the whole, will in time doubtless become the most significant part of world trade. One of the less expected results of this rising importance of invisibles may be the liberalisation of Communist society.

For trade in services may open up their economies in a way that merchandise trade never would. Already the tourist trade is so lucrative and so productive of precious foreign exhange that countries in the East are falling over one another to acquire a share. The range of contacts with the outside world for a growing number of Soviet citizens will thus grow, which means an increasing number of relationships for the secret police to supervise. Indeed big brother activities in these countries may become far too big to handle, especially when the internal growth of certain services – private telephones, for example – may be simultaneously growing too fast for the KGB to be able to digest all the information coming in from surveillance. This cheerful hypothesis is rather more convincing than the usual convergence theory (which is only inverted Marxism) that the economies of East and West are growing more alike and that therefore their political systems will merge because the West toys with dilute forms of planning while the East experiments with markets, or because the Russians have to have cars and washing machines and television sets, and therefore have to develop a sort of consumer capitalism and a similar society to the bourgeoisified West. For both the development and the swapping of services (which includes cultural and sporting exchanges) are likely to extend human contacts much more than consumer durables revolution. Not that this is meant to be another version of the tired old moral axiom that nations will live in harmony if only their peoples can understand one another. On the contrary peace is often more soundly based on ignorance than intimacy. Understanding may very well open the flood gates of hatred and xenophobia. Rather the point is that the service society and the growth of the international service economy should, at least until the electronic revolution catches up, expand the number of unsupervisable personal relationships and consequently make the Soviet societies more open to outside ideas. This in itself should provide grounds for optimism, for it is plain that where there is free competition in ideas decency and tolerance have at least the chance to prevail.

If the Communist response to the expansion of invisibles is as yet conjectural, that of many Western politicians, especially in Britain, is unambiguously opposed. Those who, at home, regarded services with distaste were no better disposed to them for being shipped abroad. In the British case some who were previously hostile are at least beginning to appreciate the bonanza which invisibles have provided for the balance of payments, perhaps because in 1970 they almost saved the Wilson government – an ironic thought in view of the tax penalties which that government inflicted on the service industries. If, then, such blindness could afflict leading politicians in a country whose invisibles account for two-fifths of total exports, it is not surprising if, elsewhere, they are appreciated even less. Indeed, ignorance alone might explain why the postwar movement for liberalisation of world trade, such a success in relation to merchandise, has with regard to many services been such a flop. Restrictions abound; at sea there are the shipping conferences, in the air there is the far more effective International Air Transport Association, in insurance and banking many countries seek to keep business in the hands of their own nationals or tolerate foreign enterprises only on very restrictive conditions. The creation of a huge free market in services is one of the Common Market's most exciting possibilities. The current fear is that in going more European it may become less international. Thus the projected common policy for insurance would hamper the worldwide operations in which Lloyds of London engage. Obviously, no country in the enlarged Community has a greater stake than Britain in the fulfilment of the Rome Treaty's promise of free movement of services, especially those financial ones from which London has so much to gain. In return, London can remedy the Community's greatest economic defect (only partly filled by the Eurodollar market, for which London in any case provides the main centre) by bringing with her the only capital market in Europe to compare with Wall Street in scale and expertise.

A free world market in services would be much more to the taste of developing countries than most of them suppose, obsessed as too many of them tend to be with the idea that, for economic development, industrial growth is the only thing that counts, an approach often allied with hostility to foreign trade, especially as import substitution is the infant industry's usual first aim. Yet, rather than pursue this policy of industrial protectionism to its invariably self defeating conclusion, many developing countries would be wise to encourage tourism, and, to that end, support the destruction of IATA restrictions, which by keeping fares up also keep tourists away. In any case, development is more likely to occur in those countries which plunge wholeheartedly into world commerce and correspondingly expose themselves to a continuous barrage of business ideas rather than in those which mentally isolate themselves in an attempt to achieve industrial self-sufficiency.

In fact, it is becoming more difficult, not less, for nations to live on their own, for, at whatever stage of economic advance it is almost impossible to avoid entanglement with the multinational corporation. Its most rapid growth has come significantly in the age of the jet airlines, and its importance may be judged from the fact that the sales of multinational subsidiaries substantially exceed the whole of international trade. They thus represent a new force in the world economy, bringing competition to bear, not only on final products, but also on the factors of production. The multinationals thus make effective, as no other institutions could, the programme of free factor movement aimed at by the European Common Market and its imitators. They also act as probably the only agencies capable of effecting the kind of economic development in the third world which results in competitive exports. They provide the channel for developing countries to contribute to multinational operations where, for example, different components are made in different countries. It is not surprising if these multinational activities arouse xenophobic reactions and the wrath of narrowminded politicians who fear that these mobile concerns too easily escape from their parochial and plundering attentions. In an obvious sense common markets are a natural counterpart to these modern hydraheaded corporate phenomena. That is not to say that common markets are necessary in order to put the multinationals down, because, as we have seen, they are complementary in function not antipathetic. Instead, the multinationals, which undoubtedly represent a new type of economic power unit, may stimulate the development of a more pluratistic world.

Indeed it is only in relatively modern times that the idea of concentrating powers in one institution – the sovereign national state – has been assumed to be the norm. It may be that the future world service society will have more in common with the great commercial civilisations of the ancient world, or, indeed, of the high Middle Ages, that is it will display a considerable variety of authorities, yet simultaneously evolve among the business community universally accepted commercial law. For the style of political authority is influenced, even though it is not dictated, by the dominant mode of production. Typically, the industrialist gives orders: the merchant negotiates. It is not merely fanciful to associate big industry with the centralised, autocratic, and insensitive use of power, nor, equally, to associate service activities with more democratic, tolerant and considerate behaviour from those holding authority. Thus, even for the economic behaviourists, the future is surely brighter than we have been led to think.

Appendix

Statistical background note to Chapter 1

International comparison of proportion of workers employed in services

Country	Year	Percentage of workers in services
Germany (FR)	1968	41.1
France	1968	45.7
Italy	1968	34.4
Netherlands	1968	51.2
Belgium	1968	47.5
Luxembourg	1968	43.3
Community	1968	40.9
Greece	1967	27.5
Turkey	*1965*	*14.9*
United Kingdom	1967	49.0
Norway	1967	45.5
Sweden	1967	47.7
Denmark	1967	41.0
Switzerland	1967	40.0
Austria	1967	39.7
Portugal	1967	31.0
EFTA	1967	45.7
Finland	1967	39.0
Spain	1967	33.3
USSR	1964	32.0
USA	1967	58.9
Canada	1967	53.9
Japan	1967	43.0

Source: *Basic Statistics of the Community*, Statistical Office of the European Communities.

Wage earners and salaried employees in services as percentage of total, 56–67, by country and type of service

			Electricity gas, water and sanitary services	Commerce banking insurance and finance	Transport storage and communication	Professional scientific and miscellaneous services
		All services				
Canada	67	61.9	1.3	20.7	8.6	31.3
	56	52.1	1.4	20.9 (61)	9.3	27.9 (61)
USA	67	61.1	0.9	21.0	5.2	34.0
	56	54.4	1.0	20.4	6.4	26.6
Japan	67	52.9	1.0	21.3	9.7	20.9
	56	52.2	1.0	18.3	9.7	23.2
Germany	67	43.9	1.0	14.0	6.7	22.2
	56	39.4	1.0 (61)	12.8 (61)	6.8 (61)	20.4 (61)
France	67	47.5	1.4	15.1	7.5	23.5
	56	42.2	1.3	11.5	7.5	21.9
Italy	67	35.6				
	56	34.5 (60)				
Netherlands	67	51.8	1.2	15.8	7.6	27.2
	56	47.3	1.2	12.4	8.4	25.3
Belgium	67	49.0	1.1	13.3	8.2	26.4
	56	42.9	1.1	9.4	8.7	23.7
Austria	67	47.9	1.3	15.8	6.8	24.0
	56	41.8	1.1	10.8	6.9	23.0
Norway	67	55.4	1.2	16.8	13.2	24.2
	56	49.8	1.2	14.2	13.5	20.9
Sweden	67	52.5	1.1	16.4	7.3	27.7
	56	50.1	1.1 (62)	16.1 (62)	7.7 (62)	25.1 (62)
United Kingdom	67	49.2	1.9	15.3	7.0	25.0
	56	44.7	1.8	14.2	7.9	20.8

Great Britain: employment in services and ten year change percentage

	Thousands		
	1969	*1959*	%
Gas, electricity and water	402.2	377.6	+ 6
Gas	125.2	133.1	− 3
Electricity	232.0	208.5	+11
Water supply	45.0	36.1	+25
Transport and communication	1,584.0	1,653.3	− 4
Railways	268.4	466.9	−42
Road passenger transport	245.6	274.7	−10
Road haulage contracting for general hire or reward	263.1	184.0	+42
Other road haulage			
Sea transport	82.6	160.4	−47
Port & inland water transport	118.7	152.7	−23
Air transport	68.6	37.9	+81
Postal services and telecommunications	443.7	310.9	+43
Miscellaneous transport services and storage	93.3	65.6	+42
Distributive traders	2,750.0	2,741.5	± 0
Wholesale distribution of food and drink			
Wholesale distribution of petroleum products	528.0	523.4	+ 1
Other wholesale distribution			
Retail distribution of food and drink	1,954.9	1,932.2	+ 1
Other retail distribution			
Dealing in coal, oil, builders' materials, grain and agricultural supplies	129.2	163.7	−21
Dealing in other industrial materials and machinery	138.0	122.1	+13
Insurance, banking, finance and business services			
Insurance			
Banking and bill-discounting			
Other financial institutions			
Property owning and managing, etc.	903.3	530.8	+75
Advertising and market research			
Other business services			
Central offices not allocable elsewhere			

	Thousands		
	1969	*1959*	%
Professional and scientific services	2,787.7	1,928.2	+44
Accountancy services	92.4	77.3	+20
Educational services	1,363.5	837.7	+62
Legal services	107.8	83.1	+30
Medical and dental services	1,001.9	736.7	+36
Religious organisations	19.8	21.7	− 9
Research and development services ⎫ Other professional and scientific ⎬ services ⎭	202.4	131.7	+54
Miscellaneous services	1,929.0	2,004.5	− 4
Cinemas, theatres, radio etc.	128.6	142.3	− 9
Sport and other recreations	68.4	52.7	+30
Betting and gambling	59.9	37.5	+60
Hotels and other residential establishments ⎫ Restaurants, cafés, snack bars ⎪ Public houses ⎬ Clubs ⎪ Catering contractors ⎭	607.9	590.5	+ 3
Hairdressing and manicure	94.0	76.3	+23
Private domestic service	118.2	304.7	−61
Laundries	86.6	129.6	−33
Dry cleaning, job dyeing, ⎫ carpet beating etc. ⎭	35.6	46.1	−23
Motor repairers, distributors, garages and filling stations	418.8	339.3	+24
Repair of boots and shoes	7.0	18.7	−63
Other services	303.5	266.7	+14
Public administration and defence	1,402.2	1,261.9	+11
National government service	567.5	515.2	+10
Local government service	834.7	746.7	+12

An OECD manpower study by analysing the percentage of workers engaged in different broad occupational categories not only illustrates the shift towards services between 1956 and 1967 which has occurred in every country studied without exception, but by splitting the service sector into its four main components helps to show whether there is any general pattern and, in particular, to discover from which subsector the dynamism of the service industries is derived. Evidently it is not from the public utilities – electricity, gas, water and sanitary services – which, in their relative demands on manpower, remained almost unchanged and in a remarkably similar range between 1.0 and 1.4 per cent of the total. The single and mild exception, the United Kingdom, which hovered from 1.8 per cent to 1.9 per cent is perhaps to be explained by the intriguing but little known fact to which Colin Clark has drawn attention, namely that the UK economy has the dubious distinction of using more fuel per unit of national product than any other country in the West.[1]

Nor again is the growth to be found in the transport subsector which, in most cases, has become less important. The proportion of workers in it is mostly around $7\frac{1}{2}$ per cent with two main exceptions. Norway's 13.5 per cent is surely the result of geography; Japan's 9.7 per cent presumably because more than most other advanced countries, she still makes intensive use of railways and therefore railway personnel with about the same length of track as the United Kingdom, on the last count Japanese railways were carrying six times as much passenger traffic and nearly two and a half times the freight.

In all cases except the United States, where there is almost no change the importance of the commerce group has risen, sometimes dramatically: e.g. France from 11.5 to 15.1 per cent; Belgium from 9.4 to 13.3 per cent and Austria from 10.8 to 15.8 per cent. A more evenly spread growth has been in the biggest subsector of all, namely professional scientific and miscellaneous services, with the UK showing the most striking increase – from 20.8 to 25.0 per cent. The only country failing to show a rise here was Japan, where there was actually a decline. This might seem odd, but for the fact that this last grouping is so varied that generalisations are dangerous. To a lesser extent this is true of the other subsectors too. For example, the transport group combines railways which are everywhere in decline with road haulage, air passenger and freight services and communications, all of which are expanding fast. Again the commerce group's

[1] *Growthmanship*, Hobart Paper 10, IEA, 1961.

growing importance as an employer, at least in Europe, is caused far more by the growth of financial activities than by either retailing or wholesaling.

Turning to the last subsector, the real pace makers are the professional and scientific services, including accountancy, educational legal and medical services, though even here there is one exception in the British case at least, namely the clergy, the only major professional group in the 'sixties in statistical retreat. A second source of growth has been public administration, which is not surprising since the 'sixties were a period of growing collectivism. This leaves a miscellaneous collection of services which, both in the United States and in the United Kingdom, have been moving at about the same pace as the economy as a whole. However, within the large categories of miscellany there are wide differences.

For instance, 'personal services' certainly appear to be of diminishing importance both in the USA and the UK. Most strikingly employment in domestic service, in the UK for instance, has more than halved in the last decade, while laundering, dry cleaning and boot repairing, if more mildly, show the same downward trend. Yet hairdressing is expanding moderately and so are motor repairing, distributing and servicing. Entertainment again is weighed down by the continuing collapse of the cinema, yet in the British case this is much more than compensated for by sport, other recreations and betting.

Index